To my loving wife, Anita ... your constant encouragement was the force that pushed me to write this book ... one page at a time

Printed in the United States of America

ISBN-13: 978-1449918392

ISBN-10: 1449918395

First Edition

The Career Journey

Table of Contents

Why read this book?.. 2

What's your pair of sneakers?............................. 7

    Go to America 7

    A pair of sneakers 9

    The mystery of the Great Pyramid.................... 11

    From WD-40 to Michelangelo........................... 12

    A common theme.. 13

    Replace Balance with Tradeoffs...................... 14

    Make Career Success a top priority 16

Determine your C-Zone 18

    Your "Talent" meter....................................... 18

    Your "Otaku" meter 20

    Your "Organizations" meter 23

    The 3 gears of your career life 25

    Zeroing in on the "C-zone" 27

    On being the "Right" person 30

Operate like a compass 34

    An obsession with Titles.................................... 34

    From Titles to C-Zones 35

    A tip from Sachin................................. 37

    From Maps to Compasses 38

Ivy League vs. ROT League 41

    De-emphasizing Degrees.................................... 41

    A Degree's true purpose in life 42

The million-dollar question 43

The 30-30-30-10 model 47

The curse of bad "mental models" 47

The 30-30-30-10 Model 50

The Ability to do the "next job level" 51

The Ability to "get along well with people" 53

The Ability to "help the boss succeed" 53

De-emphasizing education 54

The power of hopping 56

The "Fairly Successful" Fairytale 56

Blue-chips & Career Degradation 57

The "Zone of Complacency" 60

The birth of Anti-Hopping Forces 63

The All-Important "Hop Zone" 66

Don't become a boiled frog 69

MBA – Yay or Nay? 72

The MBA Drivers 72

MBA as a door-opener 73

MBA & the Age factor 74

"Replaceable Specialists" - the dead end 79

MBA & Work Experiences 80

MBA & Pay 84

Good vs. Bad Experiences 88

Leveraging Corporate Strategy Principles 88

Differentiate Yourself 91

Join Teams that deliver RESULTS 94

Go for Complex "Big Impact" Projects 95

Try to rotate through different jobs 102

The importance of failing 104

Mimic a Canadian goose................................. 106

Unleash the Change Agent in you 110

Change Agents vs. Project Managers 110

WIIFM – The magic formula of change........... 112

When the engine is running… 114

Wear the bastards down 115

Communicate often 116

The "30% Support Rule" 118

Use the foot-in-the-door technique 119

Unleash the power of personalization 120

The Power of PowerPoints.............................. 122

"Right-size" your project team 126

Watch out for Red Herrings............................. 127

A salesman & chameleon in perfect harmony . 128

Lastly … the power of stopping 129

The business of Business 133

On COGS, Fixed costs & Variable Costs…….. 134

The untold truth about "profit" 137

The fascination with EBITDA........................... 140

The "FE-BE Balance" in Value Chains 141

The "Process" advantage 148

Brand "I" Management 153

The power of branding 153

When $1 is worth more than $25000 154

An emphasis on packaging 156

A lesson from Bollywood 158

Branding the Google way 160

The state of emotional neutrality 161

Perception – the silent killer 164

Be assertive … and aligned 166

From "scripts" to "opinion coalitions" 168

Appreciating Sprezzatura 170

Take a contrarian position 172

Be unpredictable 173

The "Speak Up-Shut Up" Flowchart 174

No alibis please!!! 177

Be comfy looking dumb 177

Don't work for jerks 178

Be Funny – The "haha" type 180

Read a lot 181

The back-pocket panacea 187

References 190

Appendix 193

"*Otaku*" Discovery Sheet 194

"Companies I love or admire" 194

About the Author 197

Why read this book?

A few years ago, one of my friends graduated from a fairly good business school. He is presently an employee of a blue-chip organization with corporate headquarters in the heart of Silicon Valley. Since he joined the organization, he has led and successfully implemented some impressive projects – not ones that would create a "dent in the universe" but still good enough to raise a few eyebrows. While he is happy with his achievements so far, he is also frustrated by the lack of clarity around what to do next in order to rise up the career ladder. He finds himself unable to rationally explain why some of his peers are getting promoted and he is left behind. What did they do right or did not do wrong that made them the favorites when decisions around promotions were being made? He is on a mission to figure out the elusive formula for rising up – definitely sooner than later because his goal is to be a Vice President at the company in ten years or less!! And, that's at least three levels above from where he is at present!! Even though he believes in his abilities and has the confidence to execute the role of an executive, the path to that position seems a bit blurry....maybe even non-existent. Are you in the same shoes as my friend trying to figure out how to climb up the corporate ladder faster than the norm? Is there even a norm?

There are hundreds of books published in the area of Career Management. I have read many of them over the years and like many of you, was in search of that elusive magical formula for career success. Many of the books are gems in their own right. Each one has shared a nugget or two of good advice but at the end of the reading, I was not able to clearly put anything into a specific action plan. I was left with an author's point of view about something that lurked in my mind for a couple of weeks and then vanished with the passage of time. I realized that many readers are probably in the same shoes. The hundreds of hours spent in reading did not translate to any significant impact or change. If the time you have spent in reading a book does not bear fruit, I believe that the book has not done justice. This is where I hope this book will differ. My intent is to offer you tangible actions that you need to take at certain phases in your life. If you execute those actions, success is not guaranteed. But, I know for sure that <u>it will increase your odds of success astronomically</u>.

Over the past roughly twenty years of my corporate life in blue-chip organizations, I have seen a pattern among people rising up faster than the norm. A pattern that is latent and not obvious to the majority of experienced employees. A pattern that is definitely invisible to the rookie or newbie in Corporate America. But, again it is <u>a pattern that is characterized by the right execution at the right time at the right age and in the right way</u>. I realized that if I could go back twenty years, I would probably do a lot of things differently than what I actually ended up doing. Unfortunately, I cannot do much about that now. But, through this book, I hope to share the lessons that I have learned over the last two decades of life in corporate America. I want to share the patterns of success that I have discovered through observation, reading and personal assessment. I hope that every entry-level professional reads this book as they will find themselves equipped with the "gory secrets" of success in Corporate America – <u>without having to spend 20 years living through it</u>!! This book will also help the mid-level professional reset their baselines and maybe craft a new strategy for the rest of their lives. Entry-level professionals are likely to benefit a lot more from this book than the seasoned professional only because they have a lot more runway to implement the suggestions that I have offered in this book. That should not, however, deter anyone from reading this book as variants of the principles and suggestions that I offer in the chapters are also applicable to life outside of work. Perhaps the most important point to remember is that the principles that are shared in this book are not a fad that will fade with the passage of time. As long as companies exist and people get hired to do a job, you will find use of these principles. And, I don't see that ending for a long time to come. Alright...it's time to share my secrets. Are you ready for the journey?

Chapter 1

What's your pair of

sneakers?

"If you don't much care where you want to get to,
then it doesn't matter which way you go"
~ Lewis Carroll in Alice in Wonderland, 1865

Go to America

It was the month of April in the year 1985. I was celebrating my graduation out of High school in Mumbai, India. Formerly known as Bombay, the city of Mumbai is the second most populous city in the world with approximately 14 million inhabitants. The city is also the commercial and entertainment capital of India. I grew up in what is considered to be the classic definition of a "middle-class" family. We lived in a modest 500 square feet apartment, termed as a "cooperative society", in a busy crowded street called *Hanuman Road*. Growing up in a middle-class family has its advantages – you have a lot to aspire for. Perhaps, the only good thing about all those aspirations was that they shared one simple and consistent quality – *they were usually materialistic in nature.* When multiple problem statements are backed by a consistent attribute, it usually tends to significantly simplify the problem definition statement. In my particular situation, it was, to be more precise a problem definition question - *How do I achieve materialistic pleasures in life? And, how do I achieve them in the quickest possible manner?* India was not the answer because she was characterized by the attributes of a normal curve. There were very few rich people, few rich people, a lot of middle class people, a lot of poor people and some very poor people. Taking a course in Statistics in my second year engineering class only confirmed the odds being very low of fulfilling all my materialistic needs in record time by staying back in India. The answer to my dreams essentially boiled down to the answer to the question *"Which country in the whole world offers the highest probability of achieving material benefits in the quickest time by leveraging off good education as the backbone?"*. Answer: The United States of America. It didn't take long for the 15-year old "me" to zero in on the immediate priority – *Go to America and figure out some way to get there quickly*. Out of all the competing priorities in my life, I had finally determined the most important one. It was a relief of some sort. Exactly seven years after I had graduated out of high school, in the wee hours of August 15, 1992; I landed at the JFK airport in New York City!! With less than $100 in my pocket!!

A pair of sneakers

Among my list of favorite movies is a 1997 Iranian production titled *"Children of Heaven"*. The movie essentially revolves around a little boy by the name of Ali, who had lost his sister's pair of sneakers and how the two of them creatively come up with simple and creative solutions to run the show until their father gets his next paycheck to buy a new pair of sneakers. The film showcases the many elements of growing up in a poor family while upholding core principles and ethics. Of the many memorable scenes in the movie, played so beautifully by the two kids, one that stood out was when Ali decided to take part in a school marathon race because the "third prize" was a pair of sneakers – something that he needed very badly to give back to his sister. When his sister asked him what the prizes were for the first and second place, Ali said he did not know what they were as he had not paid attention to them. All that he cared about was the prize for the third spot – *a pair of sneakers*!! He knew exactly what he wanted with an unmatched level of clarity and focus. His priority was crystal clear. He did not care about the #1 and #2 spots and, in fact, did not want either of them.

He tried real hard to be at the #3 spot, the spot that carried the reward of *a pair of sneakers*!!

The mystery of the Great Pyramid

The Great Pyramid of Giza is one of the oldest and largest of all the pyramids in Egypt. It's height is roughly 455 feet, each base side is 756 feet long and the mass of the pyramid is estimated at 5.9 million tons. The volume of the pyramid is roughly 2.5 million cubic meters. A lot of research and studies have been done around the construction of this pyramid, with the predominant one being that the pyramid was built by moving huge stones from a quarry and dragging and lifting them into place. This seemingly simplistic explanation did not satisfy Jean-Pierre Houdin, a French architect. He left his Parisian architecture firm in 1999 to devote himself to solving the mystery of the Great Pyramid. He became obsessed by the centuries-old mystery of how the Great Pyramid was built. For ten hours a day, he labored at his computer to create exquisitely detailed 3-D models of the interior of the Great Pyramid. After five years of effort, the images on his computer screen provided evidence of the secret – a secret that the pyramid "was built from the inside". Jean-Pierre Houdin has put in roughly 20,000 hours to understand how the heck the Great Pyramid was built. I cannot think of one single hobby or activity in which I would have spent even 1,000 hours!! Can you?

From WD-40 to Michelangelo

You don't need to be a handyman to know what WD-40 is. The well-known grease is a household name that works like magic to fix squeaky doors and keep the garage door spring functioning smoothly. What Google is to Search engines, WD-40 is to lubrication. However, little do people know that WD-40 stands for *"Water Displacement – 40th Attempt"*. Norm Larsen, founder of the Rocket Chemical Company developed WD-40 in the year

1953 on his 40th attempt!!! Or take the case of Michelangelo, who endured 7 years of lying on his back on a scaffold to paint the ceiling of the Sistine Chapel.

A common theme

Whether it is the story of an Iranian kid chasing a pair of sneakers or a French architect spending 20,000 hours conceptualizing over how the Great Pyramid of Giza was built or a scientist who failed 39 times before developing the best lubricant in the world, the underlying common theme is the same. They had zeroed in on the one thing that truly mattered to them and would not rest until they achieved that goal. They had clearly redefined what "success" meant to them. The rest was simply "execution".

Replace Balance with Tradeoffs

The definition of success is a relative one. What is success to you may not be success to someone else because of differing priorities. A vast majority of people go through life without clearly understanding what matters the most to them. A clear understanding of priorities is critical because it helps you decide what you are willing to sacrifice in order to gain something. It should be remembered that the people who have been successful in corporate America have also sacrificed a lot in the personal front in order to achieve their goal. As the saying goes, there are no gains without pains. In many ways, the phrase "work-life balance" can be misinterpreted or even misused. It can be the biggest career progression killer, if not properly understood. There is technically and realistically no work-life balance. There are only work-life tradeoffs. So, drop the word "balance" and replace it with the word "tradeoffs" in order to add more meaning and realism around it. As Stephen King stated, *"Talent is cheaper than table salt. What separates the talented individual from the successful one is a lot of hard work"*. For the career minded who wish to see themselves at the pinnacles of corporate success, the tradeoff is time at work for time at non-work activities. If you wish to balance the two, say goodbye to career growth and believe that you can really get anything you want if you are willing to pay the price for it!

Make Career Success a top priority

If you are reading this book, you need to have one clear and top priority – a priority that centers on reaching the career success goals you have set for yourself. Achieving career success needs to be your *"pair of sneakers"*. If you have always wanted to succeed in your career but did not make it a top priority, then this is the point in time when you need to change your priorities in life. In order to benefit the most from this book, you have to <u>*live and breathe about "achieving corporate success"*</u>. It has to be the strategic vision of your life. The rest of the book is just executing to achieve the strategic goal you have set for yourself. It is all about the actions you need to take to make your vision a reality. There is a pretty apt Japanese proverb that I would like to share at this point ~ *"Vision without action is a daydream. Action without vision is a nightmare"*.

Below are the top takeaways from this chapter.

Tip 1: *If a successful career is important to you, then give "Career Success" the highest priority!!*

Tip 2: *Drop the phrase "Work-Life Balance" from your jargon. Replace it with "Work-Life Tradeoffs"*

Chapter 2

Determine your C-Zone

"The supreme accomplishment is to blur the line between work and play." - Arnold Toynbee

Your "Talent" meter

Once you have made up your mind that career success is truly important to you, the next logical step is choosing the path that will get you there - sooner than later. There are many paths that can lead to the end result, some short and some long, some enjoyable and some not so enjoyable, some while sticking on to your core values and principles while others may not. The frequent problem faced by many is that they do not know where to begin. I am reminded of a funny quote by Stephen Bayne ~ *"I am rather like a mosquito in a nudist camp; I know what I want to do, but I don't know where to* begin". So, the basic idea here is to zero in on the "one" path to choose to move forward with. The shortest path will usually be the one where you are really good at what you are doing. In fact, being just good may not be enough. You have to be among the very good or best at it. Hence, the first and perhaps, the most logical question to answer is *"What am I really good at?"*. You may be born with some of these talents while you may have gained other new talents with the passage of time. For example, you may be really good at playing the piano, writing cartoons, solving complex math problems, giving speeches to large audiences or strategizing. These are essentially your "**Talents**". In the book *"Multiple Intelligences"*, author Howard Gardner describes at least seven types of intelligence ranging from Bodily-kinesthetic, Interpersonal, Verbal-linguistic, Logical-mathematical, Intrapersonal, Visual-spatial, Musical and Naturalistic. This makes perfect sense—people are naturally talented at different things. One way to identify your talents is to answer questions like the ones below:

- *What subjects did I always get good grades at in school?*
- *What were those instances when people complimented me for my work?*
- *What do my friends tell me I am good at?*
- *What are some of the things that my managers have always told me consistently that I do well?*

Talents can be thought of as "tangible skills" that you possess – *whether you really like them or not, you are good at them*. Knowing where you stand in the talent meter is an important first step in career management.

Your "Otaku" meter

Once you get past the talent meter assessment, we move on to the next logical step – your passion assessment or an evaluation of the things that you really like to do. Or stated very simply, these are your "**Passions**". One way to determine your passions is to ask people who you are very close to you to help define the moments in your life when you were truly happy. I mean "happy" happy. In order to zero in on your passions, look at the activities of the past few weeks or year and see which ones you <u>enjoyed with a sense of purpose</u>. For over a good couple of decades, I developed a love for Japanese words. Why? Firstly, because they sound pretty cool. And, secondly, they seem to convey a meaning behind a message with no distorted interpretations. In essence, they are simple yet deep and powerful. Some of the classical ones that I learned as a student of Industrial engineering & later on as a student of MBA are *Kaizen, Kanban, Muri, Mura, Muda, Ishikawa, Andon, Heijunka, Jidoka, Nemawashi, Kaisha and Poka-yoke*. A new Japanese word that has become part of my lingo is *"Otaku"*. It refers to people with obsessive interests for any particular theme, topic or hobby. Jean-Pierre Houdin, who spent 20,000 hours in total to understand how the Great Pyramid was built, had an *"otaku"* for the Great Pyramid. If you are spending hours in Facebook and thoroughly enjoying every moment of it, you probably have an *"otaku"* for Facebook and social networking sites. The founder and CEO of Starbucks, Howard Schultz, stated *"It took years before I found my passion in life"*. I think it would be incorrect to just simply state that Schultz had an *"otaku"* for coffee. I bet there are millions of coffee lovers in the world, including yours faithfully. But, Howard Schultz was different. He gave coffee a new level of respect. He made drinking coffee as a reflection of "living in style". All because of one man's *"otaku"* ... it was an *"otaku"* not just for serving good quality coffee as a drink. It was an *"otaku"* for taking coffee to a different plane altogether. And only someone with an "otaku" could have accomplished that feat!! Do you have an *"otaku"* for anything? Spend at least day or two pondering over that question. Now, go back to your work and your profession. Do you believe you have an *"otaku"* for what you are doing at your workplace? There is a pretty simple test to help determine if you do or don't. That simple test is to check if you get tired at the end of the day's work. If you are truly passionate about your job, you won't feel tired because you have, in theory, enjoyed every minute of doing it. It goes without saying that every Olympic participant has an *"otaku"* for the sport they are representing. Vishy Anand has an *"otaku"* for chess, one of the reasons why he is a world champion. Sachin Tendulkar has an *"otaku"* for cricket, again why he is among the greatest batsmen in the world. Having an *"otaku"* is a prerequisite for success in your chosen career.

Your "Organizations" meter

The third and last variable that defines career success is the organization that you work for. I call this as your "second home". Maybe even your "first home", in some cases. If you are going to spend 9 hours every weekday at this place, it is almost like a home. You need to love spending the time you spend at the place you work. You need to love the organization. You have to love the culture and the leadership in the organization. For example, you may like Apple for the "cool" gadgets that they come up with and the amazing leadership of Steve Jobs; hence Apple will be part of the set of companies that you will truly love to work for. You may also admire some small unknown company, say XYZ, with less than 100 employees because you like the culture of the company and the way they treat their employees. No job or profession will ever be right for you if it requires you to work with people who don't share your values or respect you as an employee. You have to like your colleagues – and feel authentic around them. Hence, the organization and its working culture are important elements of your assessment. This is one of those variables that are *"somewhat within your control"*. The reason it is not "fully within your control" is because there could be many other factors that prevent you from being 100% flexible. You may want to live in the same city to be close to family and friends, hence limiting your choices to the organizations in that city of your choice. Hence, your flexibility is somewhat limited in that respect. But, where possible, the "Organization" should also be captured as one of the variables in your quest for career success. The greater the flexibility you have in this regard, the greater is the opportunity for success.

The 3 gears of your career life

The three meters of Talents, Passions & Organizations should constantly operate like three gears in the back of your mind at all times. These are constantly turning with the passage of time. As they turn, each one gains new perspectives and knowledge. They can also influence each other and thereby we even see a dependency relationship between them. For example, you may pick up some new hobby and suddenly realize that you have an amazing level of talent in the same too. The talent, in turn, can make that hobby your new passion. And voila, you may also find an organization that is providing the product or service that is very closely aligned to your new passion and talent. Bingo!!

Figure 2.1 – The 3 gears of your career life

Zeroing in on the "C-zone"

The three variables of Talent, Passion and Organizations taken together form the essence of the "*T-P-O Model*". If you think in terms of Venn diagrams, the common area shared by the three ellipses is the area where all the three variables are operating simultaneously. This common area is the one where your probability of career success is the highest. I call this common area the "**Career Success Zone**" or "**C-Zone**" in short. The career success zone will vary from person to person, for obvious reasons. The odds of the "*C-Zone*" to be almost identical for two randomly chosen individuals are pretty low. This is precisely why the "*C-Zone*" is, actually, quite personal. And, being personal, it makes it the unique differentiator of you from your competition. You, as a career aspirant, have a "*C-Zone*" where your potential for career success is almost unmatched by anyone.

Your skills for the role AND your love for the role AND your love for the organization makes you a compelling value-proposition!!

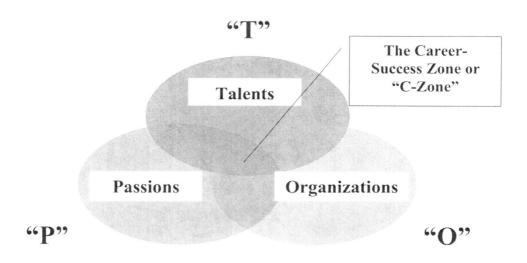

Figure 2.2 – The Career Success Zone or C-Zone

Another effective way of looking at this model is to think of these three variables as being fed to a funnel. The three variables interact with each other and finally what emerges out of the funnel is "Your C-zone" – the filtered version of the final output that takes into account the interplay between the three gears of your career life.

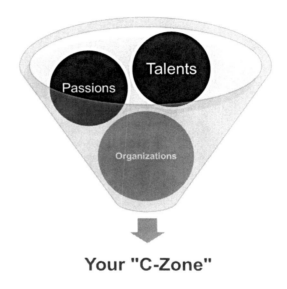

Your "C-Zone"

Figure 2.3 – The Career Success Zone or C-Zone

I am not a big believer in spending too much time in self-analysis. So, you will definitely not find a deep-dive on personality assessments, skills assessments, a custom software CD at the back of this book and all that jazz. There are plenty of books written by various authors who do a swell job at that. All I request of you is to spend about 1-2 hours in zeroing in on your "C-Zone". I do not believe it should take more than that if you really know what you are doing. There are some simple forms at the back of this book in the APPENDIX section to help you quickly determine your very personal "*C-zone*".

On being the "Right" person

Succeeding in your chosen career is essentially about being the "right person" when the right place and right time present themselves to you. The famous Irish playwright, George Bernard Shaw, was a clerk in a dry-goods store in Dublin. One day, he simply decided to quit his job and take on to spending all the time to writing plays in the city of London. His promise to himself was to experiment with this new profession for about three years. If he did not succeed in 3 years and make a living out of writing plays, he could always be a clerk in the dry-goods store again. He knew that he had a talent for writing, he realized that he had an *"otaku"* for writing and he realized that the right city to use his skills was London; not Dublin. In a nutshell, Shaw identified his *"C-zone"* and made the leap to a role that had the best overlap with his *"C-zone"*. The result: Nobel Prize in Literature, 1925!!! Imagine what the world would have lost had G.B. Shaw not taken that chance to move closer to his *"C-zone"*. The moral of the story is that your odds of being truly successful is heightened significantly by making a move closer to the *"C-Zone"*. You have no control (*well, almost no control*) over the place and time variables. When and where success will meet you is and will remain a big question mark. However, you can control if you are the "right person" for the job or significantly increase the odds in your favor by aligning yourself to your *"C-zone"*.

In a nutshell, career success is about two things:

- *Being the "right person". These are primarily governed by your talents and passions.*
- *Increase your odds of being at the right place at the right time. This is partly the organization you choose and more importantly, which group or function within that organization you are aligned with or a member of.*

We can also state this in the form of three questions that you should ask yourself at any point in time in your career life.

1. *Do I have the right skills or talents to do the job?*
2. *Do I really love this job?*
3. *Am I in the right place where the odds of getting picked for the next promotion are the highest?*

At the end of the day, there is nothing more satisfying than to have someone "pay you" for something that "you enjoy doing". In the book "Strengths-based Leadership", the authors Tom Rath and Barry Conche state "*if you spend your life trying to be good at everything, you will never be great at anything*". Very nicely put. Focus on the few things that you are really good at and where you have a passion and see how the combination works like magic. If you are going to work for the rest of your life, why not take the time to make sure that working is like playing every minute of your working life!!

Tip 3: Determine your "C- Zone" & take on a role that has the highest overlap with your C-zone ... and don't plan on spending more than 2 hours in figuring out your "C-zone"

Chapter 3

Operate like a compass

"Choose a job you love, and you will never have to work a day in your life." - Confucius

An obsession with Titles

Over the past many years, I have quizzed many friends, co-workers and students as to where they would like to see themselves from a long-term career perspective. The simple question that I posed was "What is your career goal in 3 to 5 years?". Below is a sampling of answers that I usually get from the majority of them.

- *"I would like to become a Director at my current division in 3 years"*
- *"I would like to become a Vice President in the IT department in 5 years"*

- *"I would like to become Group Lead before I am 35 years of age"*

The pattern is consistent. Each career goal statement has a "Title" and the even more aggressive ones even added a time dimension. The typical format is *"I would like to be <so-and-so> in <so many> years"*. Quite frequently, even the primary function of interest is missing. The title by itself seems to be enough to get the juices flowing. Is anything wrong with this approach or career goal? Everything!!!

From Titles to C-Zones

Approaching your career or life with a title in mind is flawed because it closes many other, probably even better, doors of opportunity. A better answer would be *"I would like to be operating in my C-zone in 1 year"*. The fundamental idea here is that if you are operating in your "C-zone", you are operating at your highest potential. And, once you are at your highest potential, it is then just a matter of place and time. There is really no need to crave for the title because it will automatically come to you even without you asking for it – at the right time.

The Bhagavad Gita, simply known as Gita, is a sacred Hindu scripture comprising of roughly 700 verses quoted by Lord Krishna. One of the quotes from the Gita is worth quoting here because of it fits nicely in this context.

> On action alone be thy interest,
> Never on its fruits.
> Let not the fruits of action be thy motive,
> Nor be thy attachment to inaction.

The underlying message is clear. Focus on action alone – the action being making career moves that take you closer to the "C-zone". The title is essentially the "fruit". It is important to detach yourself from the fruit (the "title" and the "money") and focus instead on the action ("movement to C-zone"). It is also worth emphasizing that sitting still is not a good option unless you are certain that you are sitting right on top of the "C-zone". And, if you are in your C-zone, the odds are usually pretty low that are still anyways.

A tip from Sachin

Sachin Tendulkar is a name that is known to anyone who has heard of the sport of cricket. He is considered to be the greatest batsman ever and has earned millions in endorsement deals over several years. In a recent interview that quizzed him on the secret of his success, he offered some beautiful advice that should be etched in stone by every career aspirant. Quoting Sachin, "_Money should just be coincidental. The passion and the desire is the most important thing. I worry about runs, not contracts_". The same line of thinking can be extended to success in your career. Success and money is the result. The focus and energy should primarily be in the "how to score runs" and less on "what I will get if I scored the runs". The same goes with any goal or mission in life. The fruits should always be, as Sachin says, *"coincidental"*!!

From Maps to Compasses

The famous management guru, Peter Drucker, once said *"Top Management is a function and a responsibility rather than a rank and a privilege"*. Thus, an important lesson for all new professionals is to drop the attachment to "Titles" and create instead, attachments to roles and responsibilities. In her latest book, "10-10-10: A Life Transforming Idea", management expert and author Suzy Welch makes an important point – *"Careers, by definition, don't have dead-ends. They are comprised of opportunities that lead to other opportunities"*. This is a critically important point. It emphasizes the need to manage one's career like a compass and not a map. A title-centric approach is akin to thinking of the title as "the dead end". As a young corporate professional, you should not plan for going from point A to point B in N years. Instead, your goal should be pursue along a general direction that is aligned to your C-zone. Your career compass should be pointed towards your C-zone. If you are already part of an organization or planning to join one soon, your first step should be to identify teams or functions within the organization that have the biggest overlap with your C-zone. This is where your talents and passion overlap the most; hence this is where all your energies will come into play in full force. This is the zone where you will find new meaning to your life. This is where you will find career nirvana!!

So, as we end this chapter, I would like to add two more tips to your arsenal on career management

Tip 4: Manage your career plan like a "compass", not a "map"

Tip 5: Do not get attached to a "Title". Instead, attach yourself to your "C-zone"

Tip 6: Money should not be driving force in career decisions. Money should just be coincidental. The passion and desire are the most important things.

Chapter 4

Ivy League vs. ROT League

"We spend a lot of time helping leaders learn what to do, we don't spend enough time helping leaders learn what to stop" ~ Peter Drucker

De-emphasizing Degrees

Degrees are over-rated. Let me say it again – Degrees are highly over-rated. A vast majority of entry-level professionals and sometimes, even mid-level professionals, make bad assumptions around the *"power of their degrees"*. The assumption that a MBA or a MS will automatically mean promotions or a placement on the fast track is one of the worst assumptions to make and, in fact, is a kiss of death in corporate America. Yes, I see this happen over and over again, especially amongst new graduates. I am, by no means, advocating that a degree is a bad thing. However, I would request every highly aspiring individual out there to stop flaunting their degrees or make the incorrect assumption *that a MBA degree is the best thing since sliced bread*. One of the untold truths in corporate America is that the higher up the ladder you go, the less important your education becomes and the more important your experiences, your relationships and real achievements become. You just have to see the bios of, say 50 of the top 100 CEOs in the world. Don't be surprised if a surprising number of them do not even have a graduate-level degree.

A Degree's true purpose in life

So, you are probably wondering "What the heck is the role of a degree?" or "Why even have a degree?". In my opinion, a degree is simply your ticket to an interview. In many cases, it is usually a first-level filter to get that interview. Degrees are like table stakes. *If you don't have one, you are not even in the race*. Some jobs absolutely need a MBA – so if your resume passes the electronic or human first scan test searching for that magic 3-letter acronym, you have passed the first filter. It also probably means you are one amongst 100+ other candidates who are vying to get that same job. The acid test is going to be around how you convince the person across the table as to why you are better off than the 100+ competitors who are also flaunting the same 3-letter degree. Which, essentially means, that what else do you have other than the same 3-letter bullet on your resume that "truly differentiates" you from the crowd?

The million-dollar question

Let's play a simple game. Suppose you are invited to a party and are introduced to ten random people: Susan graduated from Honolulu, Kim from Alaska, Sarah from Wyoming, Jim from Cincinnati, John from Stanford, Mike from Lamar, Sammy from Harvard, Luthar from University of Texas, Paul from Oregon Community College and Andy from

Montana State University. At the end of the introductions, I ask you the below two questions.

Question 1: Who graduated from Wyoming?

Question 2: Who graduated from Harvard?

I have not done a sampling study of this experiment. Nor do I intend do. However, if I ever did, I will not be surprised if there are more people who answer question 2 correctly than question 1. The reason is pretty obvious – _Harvard stands out_. It has a better "brand value" out there, hence it gets noticed. You pay closer attention to the name and the person who was introduced to you as a Harvard graduate.

In my simple world of classifying schools, there are only two types of schools - the "Ivy League" and the "ROT league". The acronym ROT stands for "Rest of Them". I have used the words "Ivy League" more for the power of rhyme but the essence of the message is the same. You are either from one of the top brand institutions that people notice or you are just one among the many others out there. In this definition of Ivy League are all the top branded schools like MIT, Princeton, Harvard, Stanford, Yale, Kellogg etc. The ROT League is, for obvious reasons, a very large list of every other school out there without enough juice in its brand positioning. As far as a prospective employer goes, all the schools in the ROT League are the same with no significant difference. So, if you are ever in a position trying to decide which among two ROT League institutions is a better one to choose for a MBA, the simple answer is: *"No one gives a crap"*. At least, no sensible employer or manager with an eye on the company's bottom-line is going to make the final call based on the fact that you were from brand X vs. brand Y where X and Y are schools belonging to the "ROT League". What all this means is that if you are debating over two schools from the ROT League, I would choose one with the lowest cost and the greatest convenience because

the end objective in this situation is "pure learning",
not "learning & branding".

In closing, below are two rules with respect to
degrees that every new professional should
remember.

***<u>Tip 7</u>: Degrees are like table stakes. It is
your ticket to the race. To win the race,
what truly matters is "everything else".***

***<u>Tip 8</u>: Don't waste too much time
deciding between two schools in the ROT
league. It won't matter in the long run.
Just pick the one with the lowest cost and
run with it.***

Chapter 5

The 30-30-30-10 model

"A journey of a thousand miles begins with a single step" - Confucius

The curse of bad "mental models"

In his famous book, *The Fifth Discipline*, author Peter Senge talks about "mental models". Senge states that *"Mental models are deeply held internal images of how the world works, images that limit us to familiar ways of thinking and acting. Very often, we are not consciously aware of our mental models or the effects they have on our behavior"*. If you have a poorly defined set of mental models, then chances are pretty low that you will succeed in your career. This is because you will always find your expectations not being met because of "bad operating assumptions" to begin with. It is therefore of utmost importance to redefine your mental models or assumptions so that the odds of a positive outcome are the highest. Simply stated, we have the following:

Incorrect assumptions = Unexpected results = Increased levels of Frustration

Of the many incorrect or bad assumptions that an average employee makes, one of the more dominant ones is that "*I am entitled to xxx ....*". Some typical examples of this dominant mental model are as below:

- "*I am entitled to a promotion because I am the most experienced person in this team*"
- "*I am entitled to a salary raise because it is high time*"

Getting overly attached to this "entitlement" assumption is a recipe for disaster. Let's take the example of John Salazar, a good friend and colleague. He is 40 years old and has been a project manager with the same Finance group for over 10 years now. His review over the past few years have always been exemplary and John's manager had told him on numerous occasions that he is "grooming" John for the next role. However, John's manager had not done enough socializing of the "grooming" part with his manager, the Director of the group. One fine morning, John's manager got promoted and another person was hand-picked by the Director to take over the spot left vacant by John's manager. John is therefore frustrated. The story of John probably resonates with many of you, although the contexts and exact situational aspects and the lead characters might be somewhat different. Promotions are usually the result of collective decisions. Unilateral decisions are rare in most of the well-run organizations. It should therefore be remembered that promotions and career growth only happen *when your boss and your boss's boss and "many others" think you are entitled for the same*. A better approach than feeling personally entitled to something is to truly understand what factors influence career success. This is where the 30-30-30-10 model comes in...

The 30-30-30-10 Model

The T-P-O Model of trying to determine which field and organization you need to pursue a career in is a good start in achieving career success. Drawing an analogy with a game of chess, the T-P-O model is your "Opening game". The Oxford Companion to Chess lists 1327 named openings and variants. However, a good opening game by itself is not enough to win in a game of chess. You also need excellent middlegame and endgame strategies. That will be the focus of the rest of this chapter and the book.

Over my career span of over 20 years in various roles and organizations, I have noticed four key variables that play the dominant roles when it comes to corporate success. I call this model the "30-30-30-10" model. Three of the four variables have roughly the same amount of influence in enabling career success, while the fourth one has the least amount of influence. The four variables and the % influence of that variable on your ability to succeed are as follows:

- *Ability to do the "next job level" = 30%*
- *Ability to get along well with people = 30%*
- *Ability to help the boss achieve his/her goals = 30%*
- *Educational background = 10%*

Let's quickly review each of these...

The Ability to do the "next job level"

A fairly common argument or mode of frustration for many of those left behind from a promotion is as follows: *"But I do a swell job in my current role. Then why was I left out?"*. There are two problems with this argument.

Firstly, doing a great job in the current role rarely excites a boss because that is what your boss assumed when he or she hired you. If there was even an iota of doubt that you would not do a swell job for the role that you were hired for, then you would never have gotten hired to begin with. So, your good performance in your current job is often interpreted by the boss as *"a good hiring decision"*.

The second problem is that there is a high probability that many of your peers also do a fairly good job in their assigned roles. Hence, the question goes back to you. What makes you different? If you need the next role in the ladder, *you should already be displaying the skills of that role in order to get that role*. Gone are the days when you will be automatically promoted with the hope that you will excel in your new role. There is no time or interest in organizations to take chances on an unproven skill, especially when there is a good enough supply of candidates who have already proven it.

The Ability to "get along well with people"

This is pretty much a no-brainer. If you can't work well with teams and people, chances are pretty low that you can succeed in any endeavor you pursue. At the end of the day, management or leadership is all about influencing people – whether it be getting things done or motivating or influencing or negotiating.

The Ability to "help the boss succeed"

This goal is often overlooked by the foolhardy. The person who thinks that he can outsmart and run over and above the boss is destined for failure more frequently than not. One may get lucky with some short-term wins but it can only hurt in the long-term if you tried to overtake your boss with some sneaky plan. Never underestimate the influence and power that your boss can have in shaping your career path, no matter how *"uninfluential"* your boss may seem to you. The mere position of your boss in the organizational hierarchy provides him or her with access to information much before you do – information that can be used against you, if needed. However, if you align your goals with that of your boss and constantly prove to him or her as to why you can be the most trusted advisor or ally, the odds of your success will be significantly improved.

De-emphasizing education

Education, with a mere 10% weight, has clearly been overshadowed by the first three variables. Why so? *Because once you are hired*, no one really cares about what your education is ... It is all about what you can do, how good are you to work with and how important are you in achieving your boss's goals – *as seen from the boss's eyes*. Education is always just the key to the door of the corporation. It is the first filter. Your education as cited in the resume got picked up by some smart resume filtering software or a HR person and helped you get that interview call. It's usefulness pretty much ended right there, as far as the organization goes. From that point forward, it is all about you and what you bring to the table.

Tip 9: Drop the word "entitlement"

Tip 10: The T-P-O model is like a chess opening game. The 30-30-30-10 model is part of your middlegame and endgame strategies in driving career success

Tip 11: The organization did not hire you because you have a MBA. They hired you because they believe you can show results.

Chapter 6

The power of hopping

"The path to lifetime job security is to be remarkable" – Seth Godin

The "Fairly Successful" Fairytale

One of my friends recently asked me as to what my biggest learning has been over two decades of life in Corporate America. I just summed it up in four words – *"I didn't hop sooner"*.

I have many friends whom I classify as being "fairly successful" in the career journey; however not "remarkably successful". Over the years, I have seen an unmistakable pattern in the "fairly successful" category of friends and acquaintances.

The sequence of events is something as below:

1. *Graduated from school with good grades*
2. *Took a job offer with <u>any</u> company that offered a salary greater than what they were making as a teaching assistant in the university*
3. *Jumped after a year or two to join a large "blue chip" company because the salary here was a 20% hike over the previous one*
4. *<end of story>*

I call this the "Fairly Successful" Fairy Tale, because that is precisely how it ends for the majority of individuals who play that game. Quoting Charles Darwin, *"It is not the strongest of the species that survive, nor the most intelligent, but the ones most responsive to change"*.

Blue-chips & Career Degradation

The joining of a large "blue chip" organization is a tipping point in the life of a corporate professional. It can either make you or break you – the latter scenario being more likely. So, why are blue-chip organizations a fast route to career degradation? The reasons are simple, though not explicitly obvious. In a large blue chip company, an individual's identity is lost as the role of the individual is insignificant compared to the larger organization as a whole. This should be pretty apparent to anyone, even if you have not worked for a large company. Being just one out of 100,000+ employees essentially means just one thing – *"You are pretty damn insignificant"*. When this realization dawns up the individual (which won't take too long), there are one of two possibilities the individual can do – the smart ones get out & the complacent ones stay behind. If I were to take a rough stab at the percentages, it would be something like less than 5% of the employees actually "get out" of a blue chip company to pursue other opportunities within 1 to 2 years. Also, the longer an employee stays at the company, the less likely this jump will be as new opposing forces take shape with the passage of time. This fall in probability is actually pretty drastic and the curve is asymptotic in nature i.e. it never really touches the Time axis but gets pretty close to it and stays that way for a long time. This leads to a very important concept – "The Zone of Complacency".

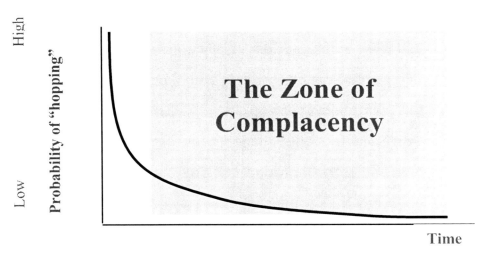

Figure 6.1 –The Zone of Complacency

The "Zone of Complacency"

The next logical question that comes to mind is "Why do individuals join blue-chip organizations and subsequently get trapped in the zone of complacency?". This can be explained by breaking down the problem into two discrete sub-problems:

- *Why do young graduates/professionals get lured to blue-chip companies?*
- *Why does complacency set in?*

The first question has a fairly easy answer. Every fresh graduate or a young inexperienced professional enters the job market with a longer list of *"have-nots"* than *"haves"*. A sample list of *"have-nots"* is something like below:

- *I do not have any experience*
- *I do not have enough savings*
- *I do not have enough $$ left over after paying off those hefty student loans*

- *I do not have a decent car to drive*
- *I can't afford the beers and margaritas*

If you get the drift, you will notice that <u>money becomes an extremely important criterion of the entry-level professional</u>. In other words, the base salary is the key driver in their decision making logic. So, a few thousands can make the difference between "accepting" or "rejecting" the job offer. Such an entry-level candidate is nice prey for the larger organizations because they can be easily lured by offering a few more thousands than the competition and if the organization plays the game just right, the new employee can be successfully pushed over to the "zone of complacency". Once that is done, the company can rest in peace and effectively take control over the reins of the horse. This provides an explanation as to what drives the young professional or entry-level graduate to blue-chips - the lure is the $$, albeit just a few thousands over the competition. The blue-chips or larger organizations easily have the muscle power to beat the small and mid-size competitors by at least $10K to $20K in base salary and that can mean a huge difference for an entry-level professional or new graduate. A simple example will help explain this difference. John is 22 years old and is an entry-level engineer who has just graduated out of a good university. He gets two offers: one with a blue-chip company at $70K/year base salary and another one with a mid-size technology company at $50K/year. The role in the mid-size seems to be a lot more exciting than the one in the blue-chip offering tremendous leadership and growth opportunities; however John still opts for the blue-chip company job because $20K was just too good to be left out, especially with the long list of "have-nots" in the list. And, with that one move, John pretty much became yet another example for the "fairly successful fairy tale".

The birth of Anti-Hopping Forces

One of the strong rationales provided by many entry-level professionals for joining blue-chip organizations is the "brand equity" that they provide in their resumes. The naïve corporate professional assumes that this job is not permanent. He is sure that he is using this as a good "launching pad" for better opportunities down the lane and won't be stuck her for too long. This is a classic case of what is also known as "*Hyperbolic Discounting*", a tendency for people to act as if the future doesn't exist or that it will be ideal. However, what John does not realize is the increase in "Anti-Hopping Forces" that will soon come into play. These "Anti-hopping forces" start roughly around the age of 25 and will continue to increase in magnitude with the passage of time.

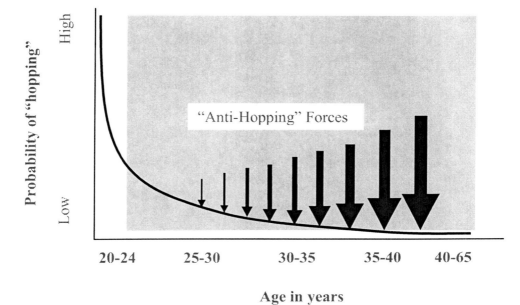

Figure 6.2 – The "Anti-Hopping" Forces Plot

The emergence of these "Anti-Hopping" Forces can be attributed to many life events that happen around the same time frame in a person's life. In the early 20's, when an employee joins a large blue-chip organization; there is a pretty quick fulfillment of the Physiological, Safety & even part of the Esteem Needs from Maslow's Hierarchy of Needs. The fulfillment of these needs in a rather rapid fashion sows the seeds for the first set of "anti-hopping forces", albeit rather weak in magnitude. The late 20's to the mid-30's is perhaps the phase in life where a person goes through the most significant changes in his or her life. In the majority of cases, the sequence of events would be marriage, first-time home ownership & new parent. Each of these key milestones in an individual's life continues to increase the magnitude of the "anti-hopping forces". By the late 30's, the force is operating at one of its peak values with kids' activities like soccer or baseball games, Taekwondo, piano practice, homeworks and state-level tests beginning to take a good load of what was essentially *free time* in the mid-20s. And, adding to this list of "To do" activities is the arrival of a new list of repair and maintenance work thanks to an aging home. Are you surprised that the word "Career" had no mind-share at all in the midst of all these other significant events? So, how do we work around this? Keep on reading....

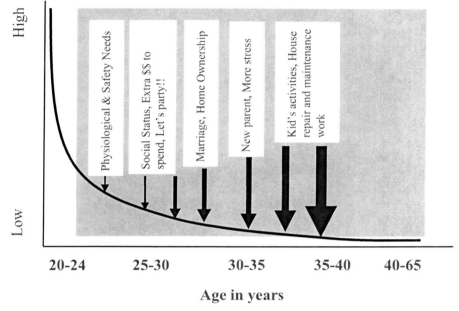

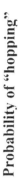

Figure 6.3 – Age, "Life events", "Anti-Hopping Forces"
& the probability of hopping

The All-Important "Hop Zone"

The "Hop Zone" is one of the most important

phases in a career-minded individual's life. This is

the phase in life that is before marriage (*assuming*

of course, that you plan to marry and fit into the

mainstream lifestyle) but after the individual has

secured a job in an organization – big or small. It is the phase where you have the highest level of independence, energy and time. This concept is more relevant for those who work for the blue-chips as the anti-hopping force of a blue-chip tends to worsen with the passage of time. In a typical individual's life, the "Hop Zone" is somewhere between the mid-20s and mid-30s. This is the zone that can make or break an individual's long-term career goals. The underlying rule is simple – "*Maximize the number of career jumps while you are in the "Hop Zone"*". The fact that you are single with less baggage also means that you have a lot fewer of the anti-hopping forces at play. This is your time to experiment and learn. This is your time to travel around the world as part of international assignments. This is your time to flood your resume with the finest bullets in terms of quality and quantity. This is your time where a failed venture can be called as a "good learning experience". Seize this time!! An expected and natural consequence of this strategy would be _a compression of events_ in the back end of the cycle. Assuming you wish to be a parent one day and still be able to run behind your kid while he is learning how to ride the bicycle or give your kid a good fight as you race Mario Kart on the Wii, the net impact of a longer _"Hop Zone"_ is quicker transitions from marriage to a new home to new parenthood. From a career success perspective, this is a sacrifice that has the potential to reap more returns than the risk. Remember, as we discussed earlier, there is no work-life balance if career advancement is the goal... Only work-life trade-offs. You trade-off longer transition periods in life events to shorter ones. What you get in exchange is a much higher potential to hit the jackpot in the career game.

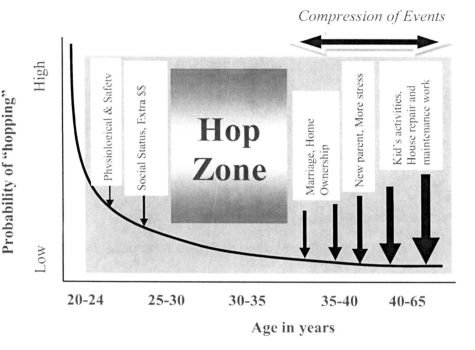

Figure 6.4 – The Hop Zone

Don't become a boiled frog

One of the well-known documented observations is that of a frog and its reaction to boiling hot water. In one instance, a frog was placed into a pot of boiling water. The frog hopped out right away, visibly shaken. There was no confusion at all on what needed to happen. In the second case, the same frog was placed into a pot of just warm water. The water was also heated on a gas stove at the same time. Surprisingly, in this second case, the frog happily kept swimming around until he was literally boiled alive. Why did the same frog lack the ability to perceive the signal of death in the second scenario? One possible explanation is that the frog was unable to react to small changes in its environment. The second and less likely possibility is that the frog was probably too damn lazy. Whatever the real reason, the moral of the story is quite simple and also adaptable to humans: *You need to be constantly on the vigil and prepared to hop even in the face of moderate changes in the environment. Don't just hop when you are thrown into boiling water.* It may be too late & you may not even survive.

I would like to conclude this key chapter with some of the most important tips in career management.

Tip 12: Define your "Hop Zone" & hop frequently while you are in the zone. Hop at least 5 jobs before you are 35 years old!!!

Tip 13: Don't become victims of "Hyperbolic Discounting"& assume that the future will be automatically ideal

Tip 14: Don't become a boiled frog. Hop and be ready even in the face of moderate changes

Chapter 7

MBA – Yay or Nay?

"Let's make a dent in the universe" ~ Steve Jobs

The MBA Drivers

Whether to pursue a MBA or not is one of the most dominant questions in every professional's mind, no matter what their age or the number of years of experience they have in their respective fields. Like many things in life, the utility value of a MBA (*or any degree for that matter*) depends on other variables.

There are four key factors that should be comprehended before the final "Yay or Nay" answer to the question "*Is pursuing a MBA worth it?*".

The four factors are as below:

1. *Your career path*

2. *Your age*

3. *Your work experience in years*

4. *Your current salary or total pay-package*

MBA as a door-opener

The first factor is your career path. Note the emphasis on the word "path". This is not an attempt to gauge if you are inspired and motivated about your end career goal. We already made that assumption in the first two chapters. The goal is to reach the *"C-zone"*. This is about your career path. This questions whether the current path leads you to the goal or not. In other words, it answers the question: *"Does my current career path take me to my C-zone in the fastest possible manner?"* A MBA can be a good degree to change your "career path" if the current path is not aligned to your C-zone, the zone where you operate at your highest level of performance. For example, suppose you have spent the last 3 years in a manufacturing operations role. However, with time, you have been extremely interested in the stock market and have also struck gold in some good investment decisions. You believe that you may have a knack at good investments and you also happen to get a good kick out of Financial Investments and Analysis. You are now pretty certain that your C-Zone is in the area of Finance. You need to carve out a new career path in Finance. You, therefore, need a change in direction. You simply cannot get there by digging your hole deeper and deeper in manufacturing operations. This is where a MBA can come to your aid. It can open a new door for a new career path that might otherwise be closed.

MBA & the Age factor

The utility value of a MBA is highly dependent on the person's age. There is an optimal age range, no doubt, wherein you will benefit the most from a MBA. Going for a MBA too early has less utility value because you do not have enough experience to truly appreciate what "corporate culture" or "office politics" or "virtual teams" or "managing upwards" truly mean. This is one reason why some of the better schools have mandatory requirements on a minimum amount of years of real work experience before they even consider students for the MBA program.

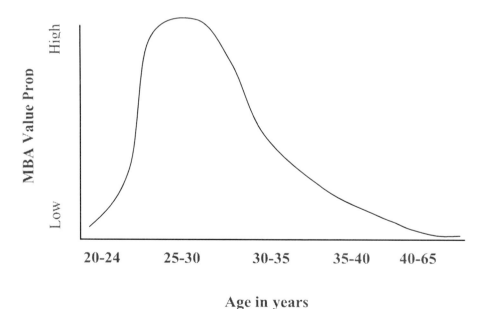

By the same argument, spending the money and the time on a MBA program after a certain point in time as measured by your age also has a decreasing value proposition; assuming that the value prop is measured by the degree's ability to put you on a fast track for career growth. Once you are in the mid-30s and beyond, you have probably become quite experienced in your profession as well as the perception that you carry in your workplace. A new degree is not going to do a whole lot in changing the way others think about you. Nor is the degree by itself necessarily going to change you in a significant way. Many professionals get a MBA degree in the late 30s or early 40s assuming that the degree will automatically come with accolades, titles and money. That's a pretty bad assumption!! Those are all the wrong reasons to do a MBA at any age. So, what is the optimal age to get a MBA? In my opinion, *the optimal age is between 25 to 30 years of age, with a higher preference for 25 over 30*. The ideal sequence of events leading to the MBA should be something like below:

1. *Earn your Bachelor's degree by the time you are 21 or 22 years old*
2. *Work for a good company in multiple rotation type roles for 3-4 years*
3. *Quit your job and pursue a MBA at a very good school as a full-time student*

The reason why the value of a MBA is astronomical in the mid-20s than the mid-30s is simply due to its relationship with the "Hop Zone" that we covered in a previous chapter. *You definitely need the MBA completed before the "Hop Zone"*, thereby giving you the marketability and runway to jump around a few times before the seriously stubborn and strong anti-hop forces come into play. *An MBA is nothing but your ticket and passport to hop faster with a higher success rate*. While I may have spent an inordinate amount of time in this chapter and book just talking about the MBA degree, I do want to also emphasize that the MBA brand value has been slowly and steadily losing its charm with the passage of time. A recent study revealed that the hottest credential today is really not the MBA. It is the Master of Fine Arts (MFA) degree. The MBA program at Harvard admits roughly about 10% of its applicants. Now, compare that to UCLA's Fine Arts graduate school which admits only 3% of its applicants. Another statistic is equally revealing. Take the example of the percent of McKinsey recruits who are MBA graduates. In 1993, about 61% of McKinsey's recruits had MBA degrees. In less than a decade after that, the percent of recruits with MBA degrees was down to 43% ~ down by a whopping 18% points. As you consider the pursuit of a MBA degree, it is equally important to keep this other perspective in mind that the MBA may not necessarily be the degree with the highest brand power. It might very well be a MFA or some other degree.

"Replaceable Specialists" - the dead end

Experienced professionals come in two possible flavors – those who know a lot about just their field of expertise (Specialists) & those who know a lot about many things in general (Generalists). The more a person stays on in the same company doing the same role for many years, the more and more the person becomes a Specialist. However, one should not confuse this usage of the word "Specialist" to mean someone who is irreplaceable. You can be doing an administrative assistant job for 25 years, but that does not make you irreplaceable. The same goes with any other job for that matter. _Very few "Specialists" are truly irreplaceable_. For example, top notch engineers and fellows in technology companies are examples of truly irreplaceable specialists because their loss is a big one for the organization. That's what being truly irreplaceable is. Your loss is a big one and it is "felt" – for a long time. If you are an easily replaceable specialist, that is the worst possible position to be in. It can be a dead-end, unless you do something about it.

MBA & Work Experiences

The relationship between MBA and Work Experience is a bit complex. The true power of a MBA depends on whether you are a "generalist" or "specialist" based on your experience obtained so far. In my opinion, _the utility value of a MBA is pretty low for a pure generalist_. This is because a generalist usually has already acquired knowledge in many functional areas. A generalist already has a fairly good understanding of the dynamics of the end-to-end value chain or is consciously making an effort to do the same. By continuing to do the same and staying on top of the latest business fads and concepts, a good generalist can easily rival a MBA any day. On the other hand, _a MBA can come in very handy for any "specialist"_. This is because a MBA will provide a specialist with exactly what the person lacks – an appreciation of the bigger picture. A MBA provides an appreciation of the interdependencies between various functions in an organization. This is exactly what a specialist needs in order to make better decisions. This is what a specialist needs if the goal is career growth and promotion. Specialists need to break away from the shackles of being specialized. In today's world, plain factual knowledge within a certain area of expertise does not have too much value (*unless you perform surgery on someone*). Information is so readily available that factual knowledge has become pretty cheap. The cost is almost zero to get information. An investigation conducted by Nature magazine found that Wikipedia and the Encyclopedia Britannica are almost equally accurate. "*The average science entry in Wikipedia contained around four inaccuracies; Britannica about three*", concluded the experts. That pretty much seals the fate of Britannica, doesn't it?   Organizations like Wikipedia, Alcoholics Anonymous (AA) & Craigslist are examples of "starfish organizations". This is a term that authors Ori Brafman & Rod Beckstrom introduced in their bestselling book "The Starfish and the Spider". In such starfish organizations, no one is in charge. Yet, everyone is in charge at the same time. They simply run by the collective and "free" intelligence of the entire population. Wikipedia is pretty much the closest thing to "a free lunch" that can one expect. The moral of the story: *Knowing just facts and information is not a skill that is seen as valuable.*

If being a factual expert has "close to zero" value, then what's left? In my opinion, just two options:

- Firstly, it is the ability to solve complex problems at work with an insight that can see inter-relationships between complex functions or groups. Employees with the ability to comprehend complex systemic relationships in value chains will always be valued.

- Secondly, for those who are not great at solving complex problems, there is one more option. As author Daniel Pink states it so nicely in his wonderful must-read book "A Whole New Mind" ~ *"When facts become so widely available and instantly accessible, each one becomes less valuable. What begins to matter more is the ability to place these facts in context and to deliver them with emotional impact"*.

So, either be excellent problem solvers or become excellent messengers of the same information. No information system or blog or website can teach you the ability to think about end-to-end value chains, the ability of systems thinking, the ability to understand the political environment and tailor the message differently, the ability to tie a tactical action to a broader strategic picture or the ability to communicate with passion and emotion that leaves a mark behind. A MBA can't teach you all of this but can expose you to some of it but most importantly, it can effectively sow the seeds for this level of thinking. Management guru Peter Drucker once quoted~ *"The Confucian concept, which the West shares, assumes that the purpose of learning is to qualify oneself for a new, different and bigger job. The Japanese concept may be called the Zen approach, where the purpose of learning is self-improvement. It qualifies a man to do his present job with continually wider vision, continually increasing competence and continually rising demands on himself"*. A MBA is in line with the Zen approach. It helps you have a wider vision. Think of a MBA as a degree that will help you appreciate "value chain" thinking. Put it simply, a MBA can transform a specialist to more of a generalist. And, *becoming a generalist is the first step towards career progress*.

MBA & Pay

The relationship between MBA & Pay is dependent on many factors – is it a full time MBA or part time? Is it an executive MBA or non-executive MBA?

There is one truth that everyone should remember when it comes to a MBA degree – *a hike in pay will only come if you join a new company after your MBA*. If you are a full-time student, the question is a moot one because you can automatically join a new company and hence can expect to see a reasonable bump in the salary as compared to the pre-MBA jobs. However, if the MBA is a part-time effort while working on a job or is sponsored by the organization you work for; then expect no salary hikes post-MBA. This is logical because as far as the company is concerned, "you" are still "you". If you now prove the worth of your MBA by implementing some remarkable projects, then the odds are higher that you may get something in the near term. However, the moral of the story is simple – *If career growth and more money are part of the reason you do a MBA, it is best to hop as soon as you finish your MBA*. Every month of delay in hopping is only delaying your career growth farther and farther. In closing this chapter, below are some key tips as takeaways...

***Tip 15**: A MBA can be used effectively to carve out a faster path to reach your C-zone*

***Tip 16**: The optimal age to get a MBA is 25. The value proposition of a MBA degree begins to recede post the age of 25 years*

***Tip 17**: Don't waste time on an MBA if you are over 40 years of age. It's better to watch your kid get his Black belt in Taekwondo.*

***Tip 18**: Once you get a MBA, hop for better growth opportunities and pay!!*

Tip 19: *Good generalists with business savvy do not benefit as much with a MBA as a true specialist*

Tip 20: *Knowing facts and information is no longer considered as a valuable skill. Remember that Wikipedia gives accurate information for "free". You can't beat that!!*

Chapter 8

Good vs. Bad Experiences

"The greatest danger for most of us is not that our aim is too high and we can miss it, but that it is too low and we can reach it" ~~ Michelangelo

Leveraging Corporate Strategy Principles

I still remember the day when I opened the package of my brand new iPod. The packaging was impeccable. Every item including the iPod itself, power cords, user guide and a sleek stand was nicely positioned in place in perfectly engineered compartments. The entire experience was something noteworthy. As a customer, I felt that I had recovered at least 25% of the value of the high price I had paid by just the sheer experience of unpacking the iPod!! A couple of years later, I read the book, "Inside Steve's Brain" by author Leander

Kahney. A quote from the book stood out: *"To Steve Jobs, the act of pulling a product from its box is an important part of the user experience, and like everything else he does, it's very carefully thought out"*. This came as no surprise to me as I could personally relate to that.

Organizations compete with each other by doing something differently, gain the mindshare of the ultimate buyers/consumers and hope to convince the buyers to buy their products at a price that will generate profits to the company. It is the same pattern of thinking with every organization – whether it be a one person street hawker selling oranges in a busy street at Mumbai or whether it be a company like Apple making and selling iPods/iPhones. What brings the true competitive advantage and makes it lasting is the way an organization ultimately delivers the products and the end-to-end processes and systems that come into play by making it extremely difficult for a rival competitor to quickly imitate.

Strategy guru, Michael Porter, states *"It is harder for a rival to match <u>an array of interlocked activities</u> than it is merely to imitate a particular sales-force approach, match a process technology or replicate a set of product features. Strategy is creating fit among a company's activities. <u>The success of a strategy depends on doing many things well – not just a few – and integrating among them</u>. If there is no fit among activities, there is no distinctive strategy and little sustainability"*. Why is this insight from Corporate Strategy so relevant in a career play? Because many of the ideas that companies use for their strategic positioning are easily transferable to the realm of the individual – with some slight modifications.

Differentiate Yourself

In his landmark article, "What is Strategy?", Michael Porter mentions about how "a company can outperform rivals only if it can <u>establish a difference that it can preserve</u>. It means deliberately choosing a different set of activities to deliver a unique mix of value." This seminal concept that drives organizational success has a key role in determining individual success too. *<u>At the individual level, the key differentiator that helps deliver a unique value to the organization is your quality and quantity of experiences.</u>* It is intuitive that the more important the role & the higher up the organization the role is in, the more important the "Experience" factor becomes. Differentiation simply boils down to separating yourself from the rest of the crowd. You do that by taking on work and projects that will help differentiate you as an employee. There are certain characteristics of projects that are truly differentiators. You play a key role in deciding which projects to pick and lead versus which ones to avoid because they are not worth your time. According to the visionary thinker and thought leader, Tom Peters, the projects that have the "Wow" brand are:

- *Projects that Matter*
- *Projects that Make a Difference*
- *Projects that you can Brag About ... forever*
- *Projects that Transform the Enterprise*
- *Projects that Take your Breath Away.*
- *Projects that make you/me/us/"them" Smile.*
- *Projects that Highlight the Value that you add....and why you are here on Earth. Yes, that Big!!!*
- *Wow projects are not hype*
- *Wow projects are an absolute necessity.*

That's a lot to digest. You don't need to memorize this list nor do you need to run every project through a check against the above list. To put it simply, you should take on a project if you believe that it will help showcase you in a positive light. Take on a project that you feel excited about because it has that nice overlap with your "C-Zone", hence will propel you forward with your highest level of energy and motivation. I have visited the Magic Kingdom at the Disney World multiple times but little did I realize until recently that many of the company's top executives disguise themselves as Donald Duck or Captain Hook in the midday parade down Main Street. Whenever new executives join the staff at the Magic Kingdom, they're required to participate in the parade. The reason: to see firsthand how what they do is reflected in the eyes of children. One of the leaders said: *"You can't take off the costume without feeling awe, wonder, amazement, and knowing that you made a difference in the lives of others"*. If that is not a "Wow" experience, what is? The bottom-line message is that you should pursue a project only if you love it and feel that doing it will give you the experience of a "Wow". If not, then just say so and get out of it. You just don't have the time to waste on "non-Wow" experiences.

Join Teams that deliver RESULTS

Teams abound everywhere. There are good teams, bad teams, energized teams, non-energized teams, passionate teams, non-passionate teams, strong teams, weak teams etc. At the end of day, what adjectives we use to describe a team is irrelevant. The only metric and common denominator that truly matters is _what the team has delivered_. As a career-oriented individual, you want to join a team that has a laser-like focus on results. Look around your company and determine which teams have a good track record of constantly implementing some really "cool" projects. You should not be surprised to see if the team is comprised of really good talented people. Go and talk to some of the team's employees. Find out more about the team's leader. Good teams have leaders who continue to invest in the team's strengths and building better working relationships among the team members. Good teams always attract the best employees in the company because the career-driven employees do not stay back in low-performing teams. Good teams are also usually very diverse in their composition because _complementary strengths are one of the key attributes of good teams_. It is fair to conclude that good teams work on "Wow" projects. Being a part of such a team will also get you "Good Experiences" – a critical requirement for you to build your skills portfolio.

Go for Complex "Big Impact" Projects

Projects can be simple or complex. Simple projects have the following characteristics:

- _Less impact to the bottom-line_
- _Fewer stakeholders_
- _Small area of focus_

- *There is nothing new to learn*
- *Lacks the buzz factor!!*

Someone still has to do them. If possible, you should avoid such projects because they do not help you move forward. Some examples of simple and "buzz-less" projects are:

- Implement a conveyor line in a factory
- Change a small process step to save 10 minutes of a 3 hour assembly time
- Drop out a non-value added activity from a process thereby increasing order cycle time by 1 hour
- Negotiate a 5% saving on a part from a key supplier

All of the above projects and efforts are important; however they lack the oomph to make you stand out. You may get rewarded with a $50 or $100 gift card and a special mention (if you are lucky) in a departmental meeting. Contrast this with complex projects, which have the below characteristics:

- Medium to Significant impact to the bottom-line, hence closely watched by the people who matter in the organization
- Lots of stakeholders – usually a cross-functional effort
- Larger areas of focus impacting many activities and functions in the value chain
- You have a lot to learn – hard and soft skills
- Has a huge buzz factor with upper management curiously intent on the status of the project
- Not many project managers want to lead it because it is complex and gray.

If you come across a complex "high visibility" project that needs a project manager, grab it and run with it. Yes, it will come with its baggage of higher stress levels and late nights but it will serve you well in the long run. And, what is perhaps the most shocking revelation that I would like to make here is that _the chances of getting a promotion are significantly higher by leading and failing (within limits) on a large project than by winning on a small insignificant one_. If you think hard, the rationale for why it is true will become pretty intuitive. It is based on the basic concept of _Risk vs. Reward_. Let's take this case by case...

First scenario – Winning in a low-profile project:
A low-profile project is one without any buzz factor or one that is not really seen by top management as an earth-shattering one. It is, in essence, also a "low risk" project from a company's bottom-line perspective. So, winning in such a project will not, and should not, generate any significant reward. If you are lucky, you may get a pat in the back or a $100 gift card. The moral of the story: Expending any time in such projects is essentially a colossal waste of time, especially if you are aiming for fast career growth. You are made for bigger and better

things in life, so it is best to avoid such projects altogether.

Second scenario – Winning in a high-profile project:
A high-profile project is one with a significant impact to the bottom-line of the organization. These are the big complex projects that many dread to take on the leadership role. Such projects are characterized by a lot of buzz and top management attention and if you did one heck of a job in taking it to the finish line, you can be assured of a good reward too in a reasonable amount of time. If you don't get rewarded in spite of this, it's a signal to hop.

Third scenario – Failing in a high-profile project:
This is perhaps the most interesting scenario of all. The project is high-profile and hence, by definition, carries a lot of business risk with it. Why is it that many project managers who actually fall in this last scenario also end up getting promoted at the end

of it? A concrete example will help shed some light here. Let's consider a 3-year and $100 million ROI project with over 500 overall team members as part of the same. The project is completed successfully, however its get delayed by 6 full months in its final implementation. Hundreds of meetings and conference room pilots are held as part of this project implementation. Even though the project has technically failed in terms of budget, time and cost; the project leaders get a lot of accolades and potentially even a good promotion in 3-4 months. Are you surprised? The rationale is actually pretty simple if you go back to the 30-30-30-10 model. A high-profile project gives you ample time and opportunity to showcase yourself in the "30-30-30" part of the model. Here's why...

- You get a great chance to show that you have the maturity and capability to handle the next role

- You get a great chance to build relationships and work with people, especially with people who matter
- Lastly, it helps you showcase your boss in a good light because ultimately your success is your boss's success too. And, success here is usually seen as the completion of the big project, albeit it was finished late.

The most important point to be remembered here is that _the failure of a high-profile project is not seen as a failure of you as a person._ Top management usually tends to treat them separately. One is the project. It failed. And, there could be hundreds of reasons why it failed that are not attributed necessarily to the project leader. With ample time and opportunity to tap into the "30-30-30" portion of the model, the project leader in the end comes out extremely successful as a result. The moral of the story is simple: _Go for big, complex and earth-shattering projects that will show their impact to the_

company's bottom-line because project success and
project failure will still result in a reward for the
project leader!!!!

Try to rotate through different jobs

Job Rotations are excellent examples of "good experiences" because it moves you more and more towards a generalist. A job rotation helps you to *apply your proven skills and past experiences to a new area or function*. In this respect, a job rotation can provide you with better opportunities to outshine the existing members of the new team. The logic is simple. The members of any function are usually used to a certain way of doing things as they have been performing that role for a long time. As a newcomer from a different function, you bring to the table potentially "different and better ways" of achieving similar objectives. The result: Cool wins and a positive image building opportunity. Another reason for a job rotation is to grow yourself horizontally and become better-rounded in your skills. While you consider rotations, keep the following in mind:

- Do not lose sight of the C-zone; good rotations take you closer to the C-zone or keep you in the C-zone
- Do not rotate just for the sake of rotating – Patience is a virtue when it comes to job rotations. Pick and choose the right ones.
- Assess the ability of the job rotation to offer you with "Wow" projects i.e. the opportunity to be remarkable and make a dent in the universe

Quoting one of my mentors, "*Experience is not about the number of years on the job. It is ultimately all about the number of different kinds of cool jobs and juicy assignments that you have done*".

The importance of failing

I have rarely come across successful people in any walk of life who have not failed at some point in their lives. Failure is a critical requirement for success. Some of the greatest success stories have been born out of total failure. The author, J.K. Rowling, is a classic example. In an address to the graduating class at Harvard, the famous author of the Harry Potter series quoted: *"I was as poor as I could possibly be in modern day Britain without being homeless. You might never fail on the scale I did. But it is impossible to live without failing at something, unless you live so cautiously that you might as well not have lived at all – in which case, you fail by default. You will never truly know yourself, or the strength of your relationships, until both have been tested by adversity. Such knowledge is a true gift, for it is painfully won, and it has been worth more to me than any qualification I have ever earned"*. The more the jobs you change, the more the risk you take, the more the failures that you can experience and thereby the greater the number of good experiences that you gain in the process. In the world of the sport of cricket, Sachin Tendulkar is a name to reckon with. In the year 2010, he completed twenty years of playing international cricket – a feat by any measure of success. When asked what he remembered the most of those twenty mesmerizing years of cricket, Sachin's answer was "*I remember things clearly. I remember most of my dismissals and I don't think any cricketer forgets that*...". The eminent physicist, Niels Bohr, once stated "*An expert is a man who has made all the mistakes which can be made, in a narrow field*". If you wish to be known as a great strategist, you should have failed in enough strategic formulations that you are now aware of a lot of the pitfalls. If you wish to be known as a great change agent or project manager, fail in enough of them and learn from each of them. Failures teach us "what not to do" – an important element of a good experience.

Because once you have a solid comprehensive *"what not to do"* list, the decisions you make or actions you take have a much higher probability of success.

Mimic a Canadian goose

A few months ago, I came across an episode in the Discovery Channel that centered on the migration of Canadian geese. These birds are well known for their seasonal migrations & the V-shaped flight formation. However, if one observes closely, the front position is rotated at periodic intervals because flying in the front consumes the most energy. So, while one plays the role of the leader (the "front position"), the rest of them follow with less energy consumption. This V-shaped flight formation with rotating leaders is a key attribute to the success of their long migrations. Every bird has to be a leader at some point. If not, the migration fails. No bird puts the faith blindly on the same bird for a very long time. However, when it comes to us as employees, we tend to put a lot of faith on the same leader for too long. We stay within the confines of our role and group and just hope that our leader will hang in there. If the leader we pick is expendable, tough luck. And if a new leader comes in and finds you expendable, that's even worse. Because you have never tried to move to the front position and lead, you really don't know what it takes to lead. You have just followed the front bird all these years. You have played it too safe. That's an extremely risky strategy. And, this is no different for organizations too. Just take a look at Sony and how the competition erased its foothold in many sectors. Apple took over portable music players, Microsoft and Nintendo in gaming consoles, Cisco's Pure Digital in the video recorder market and Amazon's Kindle in the e-reader market. One of the primary reasons for Sony's failure has been attributed to its tradition-bound mentality, one that remained too focused on building excellent analog machines in an increasingly digital world. Sony played it too safe. It did not take chances. Take the example of the well-known laundry detergent, Tide. Over a third of Tide sales come only from Wal-Mart. Without Wal-Mart, Tide is a dead brand!! That is a scary position to be in. So, in a nutshell, learning to lead is very important. Don't play it safe. Move to the front, whenever an opportunity comes along. Or create opportunities where you can be in the front. Some key takeaways from this chapter follow...

_Tip 21__:_ _**Establish a difference in you that you can preserve and thereby beat your competition**_

_Tip 22__:_ _**Experiences are more important than Education; hence focus on the "quality" and "quantity" of experiences**_

Tip 23: Join teams that deliver results

Tip 24: Don't spend time in projects that do not "Wow" you

Tip 25: Remember that as long as the project is a big one with a "Wow" factor, you will benefit whether the project succeeds or fails (as long the failure is within reasonable limits)

Tip 26: The failure of a highly visible project is not perceived as a failure of you as a person

Tip 27: Don't play it safe. Mimic a Canadian goose.

Chapter 9

Unleash the Change Agent in you

"It is not necessary to change. Survival is not mandatory." – W. Edwards Deming

Change Agents vs. Project Managers

Over the past decade, Corporate America has seen a new breed of professionals doing a swell job at marketing themselves as specialists in a niche area called "Change Management" or "Management of Change (MOC)". Sometimes, change agents are used synonymously with project managers but the really *serious-about-the-lingo* types do not hesitate to call out the difference. Project managers focus on managing a project end to end – from scope, design, development, test, train and launch – all while keeping an eye on cost and time to deliver. Thus, a project manager is usually more "execution focused". Tell me what to deliver, by when to deliver, under what cost constraints and what resources do I get to make that happen. That's a project manager mindset. The change agent, however, is a different breed altogether. A change agent's mind thrives on the question "What is not working right and needs to change?". A change agent is, first and foremost, a solid and creative thinker. The change agent's forte lies in identifying the change needed to drive some meaningful sustainable and competitively advantageous difference and then driving the necessary steps to make that change a reality. Using the services of a professional project manager could be one of the many steps that a change agent may also consider, if the agent's time is better spent somewhere else. Thinking alone does not help drive change. Change agents are also fantastic leaders. They know how to get people inspired, motivated and ready for change. They use strong rationale and objective reasoning to drive home the message for change. *Every change agent is usually also good at project management but the reverse need not be true.* Good change agents are essentially good leaders too. I would like to borrow a nice definition of leadership quoted by Warren Buffet ~ *"A leader is someone who can get things done through other people"*. That is precisely what change agents have mastered too. Good change agents are hard to find. It is no surprise because the good ones climb up the corporate ladder faster than the rest. Moral of the story: *If career success is important to you, focus on being one awesome change agent*!!

WIIFM – The magic formula of change

It never ceases to amaze me when I see professionals who consider themselves to be ace presenters and change agents go up on stage and deliver a speech that very generously uses the word "I" at least 20 times in the speech. Remember the fundamental truth in driving change anywhere, whether it is an organization or even life in general: *No one cares about what you want. They only care about what they want.* They are investing the few minutes of their life to listen to you hoping that you have something to say that can positively impact their lives. Every recipient of your change message comes to the podium with just one question in his mind – <u>*What's in it for me?*</u> , better known by its acronym version, **WIIFM**. If you cannot convince your audience as how they will benefit by listening to your message for change in 3 minutes or less, you have essentially lost them. They will "hear" you out but not "listen" you out. Good change agents know the prime motivation of their audience. They know their hot spots, cold spots, weak spots, hard spots ... you name it. They know exactly what to say and what not to say in order to get the audience charged up. They realize that time is precious and this message has to come out quick.

They know that WIIFM is the magic formula to be an effective change agent.

When the engine is running...

There is a real story that revolves around a famous heart surgeon in Mumbai (India) who had taken his car to an auto repair shop. An auto mechanic in the shop was removing the cylinder heads from the motor of a car when he spotted the famous heart surgeon, who was standing off to the side, waiting for the service manager to come to take a look at his car. The mechanic shouted across the garage, "Hello Doctor! Please come over here for a minute." The famous surgeon, a bit surprised, walked over to the mechanic. The mechanic straightened up, wiped his hands on a rag and asked argumentatively, "So doctor, look at this. I also open hearts, take valves out, grind them, put in new parts, and when I finish this will work as a new one. So how come you get the big money, when you and me are doing basically the same work?". The doctor leaned over and whispered to the mechanic, *"Try to do it when the engine is running"*. Being a change agent is no different. You have to be able to drive remarkable change in the organization – all while the engine is running i.e. without creating any disruptions to the business.

Wear the bastards down

As the presenter of a new idea, you need to be totally sold on it and have an extraordinary level of commitment to the same. In the excellent book, "The Pursuit of Wow", the author Tom Peters writes: *"People can smell emotional commitment (and the absence thereof) from a mile away. Have a bull-dog persistence on issues that matter to you. That would wear the bastards down. It's not just that commitment counts in the "real" sense of your willingness to go the extra mile, it also counts in others' perception of your willingness to battle on (and on...) – they wisely choose another piece of turf to fight over"*. Your commitment to an idea is reflected in every action of yours. It is reflected in the energy and passion you display. It is contagious. People can see it, hear it, smell it and feel it. And, once they realize that your commitment is far greater than their ability to stop it, they will get out of your way. And, over time, they will even join you in the effort as everyone by their very genetic makeup wants to be part of a winning team.

Communicate often

Research has shown that the closer people get to achieving a goal, the more the effort they exert to achieve it. In other words, people will be more likely to stick with programs and tasks if you can first offer them some evidence of how they've already made progress towards completing them. What does this mean in the bigger scheme of things as a change agent? It means that frequent communication on status updates and small wins is critical to success. I have seen often projects fail or project managers losing credibility in the eyes of management by the total lack of communication on the status of the project. Rarely will you be blamed for over-communication, but be assured that criticisms will pour in like crazy for under-communication. More than any other reason, over communication is the best hedge against a colossal screw-up of the project. If you had taken the effort to keep more people in the loop on what is happening, the failure can then be branded more as a "collective failure" instead of an "individual failure". Last but not the least, always remember the old French saying ~ *"Change is a door that can only be opened from the inside"*. People are motivated to take action when they reach their own conclusions. And there is no better vehicle in opening the change door from the inside & motivating people to take action than communicating often!

The "30% Support Rule"

When people are uncertain about a course of action, they tend to look outside themselves and to other people around them to guide their decisions and actions. Robert Cialdini talks about this method of persuasion in his classic book *"Influence: The Psychology of Persuasion"*. He calls it as the Principle of Social Proof. This is precisely why McDonalds has a slogan of *"Billions and Billions served"*. If billions have eaten there, then it must be good and an average person is happy with using that social proof for making his decision to eat at McDonalds. The good change agents use this principle very effectively. If the change agent has to sell the idea to a group of stakeholders or key management folks, he does not surprise all of them with the novel idea for the first time during the final pitch. That can be a disaster. Instead, a truly remarkable change agent first sells the ideas to some of the key invitees separately in an offline one-on-one meeting. The change agent gets their agreement to vocally support the pitch so that anyone who is one the fence in the meeting becomes a victim of the principle of social proof. I have a simple thumb rule – _For every 10 people in the room, try to get at least 3 key people sold on the idea prior to the pitch and offer you the support needed to influence the unsure ones_. I call this the "30% Support Rule". Apply it and see how magically your ideas start becoming accepted without much conflict.

Use the foot-in-the-door technique

Large projects that have the ability to wow others usually have a lot of milestones along the way. Sometimes, even reaching the next milestone can be a few weeks (if not months) away. One effective way to keep the momentum and motivation alive in the project team is to adopt the _"foot-in-the-door technique"_. Essentially, what this means is to set much smaller task-oriented goals that the owners will have no excuse or problem to not complete. In other words, good change agents keep the team's focus on small wins in the immediate short-term. They realize that _the momentum generated by small wins will help propel the team with much greater intensity towards the larger goal of the team_. As Confucius said wisely _"A journey of a thousand miles begins with a single step"_. And, as small wins keep happening, the change agent ensures that a swell job is done in the communication of the wins to the team and a broader audience.

Unleash the power of personalization

Why is Google a success? Because even though the search engine serves a hundred million consumers, every search experience is still _"personalized"_. It met a personal requirement of a customer which only that particular customer wanted at that point in time. That's precisely why Post-It notes work like magic too. Research has shown that the employee motivation and satisfaction was significantly higher when a handwritten Post-It note was received from the employee's manager in lieu of an email. Consumers now spend nearly as much on decorative (and nonfunctional) faceplates for their cell phones as they do on the phones themselves. The ringtones market is a $4 billion market !!!! Again, it is all about personalization. Odwalla juice is another nice example of what a personal touch is all about. The company has *an "Enjoy by <date>" in its bottles; not an "Expires on <date>"*. The words *"Enjoy by"* are more positive, active, vibrant and beautiful. On the contrary, the words "Expires on" is dull, boring, implies death and negative. It is all about how you want to sell your next big idea.

What does all this mean to you as a change agent? As a matter of fact, quite a bit. For starters, personalize the project name. Take some time to think through a good creative name for the project. A good title for the project is a great way to connect with the team and stakeholders. By using an unexpected title or name for a project, you might foster a sense of fascination, attraction and support for it. As a general rule, _people are drawn to "cool sounding" projects and are naturally drawn to them_ – so a personal touch and a bit of creativity can go a long way.

The Power of PowerPoints

It took Galileo decades to persuade people that light objects fell as fast as heavy ones. Would it have been easier for him to persuade if he had given a pitch using a PowerPoint presentation? It is an important question to ponder over. The truly remarkable change agents know the power and limitations of PowerPoints and how to use them smartly to achieve the intended goals. Below are some of the hand-chosen tips in giving presentations:

- Keep your slides simple. The idea here is to persuade your invitees, not to perplex them with complicated analysis and formulas that only you and a small percent of population in the world fully understand. _Your goal should be create that "aha" moment for the listeners_ who have made the special effort to give some of their time to listen to you.

Dwight Eisenhower told his speechwriters *"If you can't put the bottom-line message on the inside of a matchbox, you're not doing your job"*. The same goes with presentation ideas. Keep them simple and have a bottom-line message that is not more than 2-3 simple sentences long.

- The marketing guru and fantastic author, Seth Godin, has coined a word called *"ideavirus"* for ideas that spread. Such *ideaviruses* have a higher chance of succeeding than those that don't spread. Make your PowerPoint pitch an *"ideavirus"*. Your goal is to transform every individual in the room listening to your pitch to become a seller of your idea. And to do that, your pitch needs to be remarkable and yet simple. It is a fine balance. In order to make your presentations into *"ideaviruses"*, you also need to be an effective storyteller. We have always grown up listening to stories. The well-known English novelist, E.M.Forster, pointed out the difference between a fact and story beautifully. To paraphrase his famous observation, a fact is *"The queen died and the king died"*. A story is *"The queen died and the king died of a broken heart"*. Huge difference!! The "dying of a broken heart" made the fact into an *"ideavirus"*!!

- Research data has shown that the vast majority of wine drinkers are unable to tell the difference between a $20 bottle wine and a $100 bottle wine. Stated differently, $80 delta is the value of "mental perception". We are paying an extra $80 to let our minds fool us that we are indeed drinking some awesome wine. Or maybe we are paying an extra $80 as a means of packaging ourselves to the intended audience – be it friends or colleagues or relatives. It is no longer about the taste. It is all about impression management. However, unlike wines, good PowerPoints do taste a lot better than bad ones. Good presentations are good, bad presentations are bad and the remarkable ones are remarkable. The difference can be seen and perceived by every member of the audience.

- Never forget that _the goal of the presenter is to change people's minds_. It is to gain agreement. With the exception of a few, the general rule is that people are "loss averse" i.e. they are first interested in avoiding losses than acquiring gains. Suppose you have a brilliant idea that would save a million dollars for the company and have put together a proposal to gain agreement from the stakeholders. You could pitch the idea in two possible ways:

a. _"Implement the idea to save $1 million dollars"_ or
b. _"If we do not implement the idea, we will lose $1 million dollars"_

By the principle of loss aversion, the second approach is a better one and is more persuasive. People want to avoid losses at any cost and their minds are usually programmed to operate with that line of thinking.

"Right-size" your project team

The success of any change initiative is significantly influenced by the size of the team. A team smaller than what is needed can end up being ineffective and inefficient because the team will be unable to make decisions fast enough & thereby lose costly time in the process. On the other hand, a team that is larger than what is needed can also be ineffective and inefficient because too many team players can translate to an excessive number of opinions thereby leading to delayed decisions on open action items. It is worth remembering the saying "*A camel is a horse designed by a committee*". If you need to design a horse, just get enough team members to design the horse – no more, no less. If you violate this cardinal rule, you may end up with a camel instead. It takes a certain level of good judgment and experiences to right-size your team. And, this is a critically important step...

Watch out for Red Herrings

Whoever coined the phrase "Red Herring" must have been a genius. A Red Herring is an idiom that refers to a device that intends to divert the audience from the truth or an item of significance. As a change agent for many years, I have seen red herrings all the time. They come in various shapes and forms. Some of them use Red Herrings to see you fail while others may use them as effective defense tactics. If you closely observe the dynamics, there will be an attempt by these sly players to change the core topic to something different and thereby get the spotlight away from them or away from you, depending on what their motive is. Such players will try to make meetings unproductive and delay the accomplishment of the meeting's objective. Make sure that you don't become a victim of such Red Herrings.

A salesman & chameleon in perfect harmony

Good change agents have to be good salesmen. And the good change agents realize the importance of the selling aspect. It is one thing to just solve specific organizational problems but a totally different thing to be able to sell the solutions effectively. The successful car salesman at a BMW or Benz showroom knows the difference between "selling a BMW or Benz" versus "selling a BMW or Benz <u>lifestyle</u>". The Benz salesman knows that a prospective customer to the showroom is not there to buy "a Benz". The customer is trading his money for "a lifestyle" that fits with his or her position in society. And buying a Benz is simply one of the many ways he is buying "that lifestyle". Similarly, a Kia salesman knows that a customer is in the showroom for "a value oriented" shopping experience. A Kia customer walks into the showroom thinking "How can I go from point A to point B and spend the least amount of money in doing the same?". So, while they are both salesmen at the end of the day, the strategies and tactics adopted in selling have to be significantly differently. Along the same lines, good change agents know the difference between selling it to the worker bees versus selling it to the execs. And, unlike a car salesman who is often specialized to a certain breed of customers, a good change agent may need to adapt to different scenarios and stakeholders with ease. In summary, a good change agent has to be a good salesman and a chameleon wrapped into one package.

Lastly ... the power of stopping

A vast majority of process re-engineering professionals or the so called "process experts" associate change with starting something new or different. The notion that to be a change agent means to "start" something is the worst assumption to live by. One should never underestimate the power of simply "stopping" many of the ineffective and "non-value added" processes. As the famous management guru, Peter Drucker, once stated in a rare interview *"I would ask managers and leaders what they have stopped doing in the last months"*. This is a powerful insight and something that is not pursued with the same vigor and passion by many organizations as they redesign business models in the face of new competitive pressures. So, as you wear the hat of a "change agent", never lose sight of the question: *"Can I stop doing something?"*

Key takeaways from this chapter are as below:

Tip 28: Focus on being a change agent; not a project manager

Tip 29: Remember the magic acronym to drive any change .... WIIFM

__Tip 30__: Remarkable changes need to be driven while the organization's engine is running

__Tip 31__: Have a bull-dog persistence on issues that matter to you

__Tip 32__: Communicate often – upwards, laterally & downwards

__Tip 33__: Adopt the "30% Support Rule" as an influencing tool

__Tip 34__: Generate momentum by focusing on "small wins"

__Tip 35__: Strive for personalization

Tip 36: **Make your PowerPoint slides an "ideavirus"**

Tip 37: **Right-size your project team lest you end up with a camel instead of a horse**

Tip 38: **Watch out for "Red Herrings"**

Tip 39: **Be a good salesman and a chameleon at the same time in order to be an effective change agent**

Tip 40: **Never lose sight of the question: "Can I stop doing something?"**

Chapter 10

The business of Business

"Everything that can be invented has been invented"
– Charles H. Duell, 1899, U.S. Commissioner of
Patents

There are hundreds of books that talk about the business of Business and how companies make money. However, it is rarely self-motivating to pick up a mammoth textbook on Finance or Management Accounting or Corporate Strategy. The purpose of this chapter is to share with you what I believe are some of the concepts that you should always keep in your back-pocket as part of your arsenal. Some of these concepts are strictly "theoretical" that you can possibly learn from any business school Finance and Accounting text. However, there are many concepts that can only be learned on the job after years of experience. I believe that these concepts are key for any business professional, no matter which particular area you would like to lead down the road. An entry-level professional may have a significant edge over his competition by having a strong grasp on these fundamental business and finance concepts. A quick read of this chapter should help shave a few years of "on-the-job" learning for you.

On COGS, Fixed costs & Variable Costs....

Every entry-level corporate professional, will sooner or later, be greeted with a barrage of new financial words – ranging from revenue, margins, net income, COGS, operating profit or income, gross profit, expenses etc. As an aspiring leader in your organization, you need to have a fairly good understanding of these basic foundational concepts because top management talk will revolve around these terms a whole lot. The goal of any for-profit organization is to "make money". Money is made when what the organization gets in from selling products or services (_Revenues_) is greater than what it spent as a whole in making those products or services (_Cost_). So, "Revenues" are essentially money made from "Sales". After the organization subtracts the "Total Cost", what is left is essentially "_Profit" or "Margin_". This is the basic guiding formula behind every business. Even a street hawker selling apples and oranges knows of this basic formula in order to earn his daily bread.

To dissect an organization's performance and analyze it better, there was clearly a need to break down the elements to a higher level of detail. The "Total Cost" did not help a whole lot in understanding the behavior of costs at a deeper level. Management needed more details and so did Wall Street analysts. So, there was a need felt to break down Total Cost into two buckets: A "Variable" portion and a "Fixed" portion. The _Variable Cost_ is that portion of the total cost envelope that varies directly with the production of every unit. This was directly attributed to the unit itself and discarded the rest of the costs that would have been incurred anyways (*even if the unit was not produced*). Every time you manufacture a unit, you will incur an incremental variable cost that is attributed to the unit. In other words, Variable cost "varies" with the production levels. *Fixed cost*, on the other hand, is what would be spent anyways and is beyond the company's control at least for the short-term. The rent and electricity bills paid for the buildings, the salaries of the permanent workforce etc. are all part of the fixed costs. This is also sometimes known as *"Overheads"*. As a young professional, you need to have a basic understanding of the cost umbrella and how the total cost envelope is broken down into its fixed and variable portions. Another important and sometimes confusing terminology is the difference between *"Operating Expenses"* and *"Capital Expenditures"*. The former reduces profits immediately while the latter spreads it over many years or accounting periods using a technique called *"Depreciation"*. The techniques used for Depreciation and the selection of the right one is, for all practical purposes, best left to the accounting guys. From your perspective, knowing the terminology and the high-level implication should be good enough.

The untold truth about "profit"

Most of us are aware of the three financial statements used to manage any organization – *the balance sheet, the income statement and the cash flow statement*. The balance sheet is a snapshot of the company at a certain point in time while the Income Statement is a reflection of how the company performed over a pre-defined time horizon. If you have never seen a Balance Sheet or Income Statement, I would highly encourage you to do the same. While these statements are good tools to understand the performance of an organization, it is even more important to have a true appreciation of how much *"estimating"* goes on in these financial statements. *Accounting is a lot about estimating.* For example, something as basic and fundamental as "Revenues" is by itself an estimate because it is recorded in an income statement based on deliveries, not actual sales. The dollars from the sales have not yet shown up in the door but the accountant makes an assumption that they will. So, guess what behaviors can this drive in companies who wish to portray to the market that they are growing significantly in terms of top-line growth? Another good example of estimating is in "Capital expenditures". This is also an estimate because it depends on which of the many possible depreciation methods the accountant decides to finally use. And, each of them can change the dynamics of the current quarter's bottom-line significantly. Similarly, there are many other items in the balance sheet and income statement that are technically just plain "estimates". So, what does all this mean and why should you care? As a career aspirant, this knowledge is important because you begin to better appreciate the dynamics of a business at work. You begin to appreciate the fact the revenues reported are in reality an estimate and some of the cost elements are also estimates; hence *the final "profit" reported in the income statement is also really an estimate*. It is an estimate arrived at by making a lot of assumptions along the way, hopefully without violating any of the laws of GAAP (Generally Accepted Accounting Principles). *This is precisely also why some companies can be extremely profitable on paper but may be struggling to pay the bills.* In fact, some may even just perish in a highly profitable state!!! Since so much of estimating goes on in financial statements, another natural need took birth among analysts and management – a need for a statement that is devoid of any "estimates". The answer was simple: "Cash-Flow Statement".

The fascination with EBITDA

EBITDA is an interesting and useful acronym in the field of Finance and Investments, hence requires its own dedicated section. It stands for *"Earnings Before Interest, Taxes, Depreciation & Amortization."* Irrespective of whether you go for a MBA or not, you should know about EBITDA and why this value is particularly significant in the eyes of many savvy investors and top management. Many understand what EBITDA is but the underlying rationale as to why it was developed to begin with is not that apparent. *At the heart of the EBITDA creation is an attempt to remove every element that is an "estimate" or has no relevance at all to how effectively the company managed its operations.* Taxes, Interest, Depreciation and Amortization are four such values. None of them have any usefulness or role in reflecting the true ability of an organization in managing its operations. This is precisely why the concept of EBITDA made perfect logical sense for the astute analysts. The idea was simple – the lower the number of estimates in the influence of the final number, the "purer" the value is and the less the subjectivity around it. So, remember EBITDA and its power as a financial metric and why it has a special place in investing and valuation parlance.

The "FE-BE Balance" in Value Chains

The majority of companies are essentially in the business of making something "tangible" in the form of products. Just enter Wal-Mart and you know what I am talking about. It is not uncommon for an entry-level professional to be greeted with the concept of products and its more common way of existence in the form of SKUs or Stock-keeping-units. However, what is sometimes not clearly apparent to young professionals is that the "productizing" strategy which fundamentally answers the question *"How many products or How many SKUs should the company offer?"* is a pretty complicated decision. There are two opposing forces at play – Front-End forces and Back-End forces. Balancing these two forces is key to a successful product strategy. I call this the *"FE-BE Balance"*, short for *"Front End-Back End Balance"*. More on this now ...

Front-end (FE) functions broadly refer to all those functions that interface in some way or form with product promotion & product presentation to the end customer. Marketing and Sales functions predominantly operate in this space. Both these functions can sometimes get obsessive about "pleasing" customers, with different personal motivations and agendas. Talk to any Product Marketing manager and you will see the pride of ownership with the product(s) they manage. A typical marketing manager thinks along the below lines:

- *"I want to meet all the requirements of my customers, so everything will be offered from a marketing perspective"*
- *"I don't care if the demand is too low, it still meets the needs of some customers"*
- *"These are my products and I want to showcase all of them".*

Too frequently, marketers also tend to be overly optimistic about the product line. Next, let's look at the typical sales guy mentality. The key motivation for sales folks are the commissions they earn, usually as a % of revenue generated. So, sales folks in general love many products and SKUs because it enables them to play with the pricing lever more effectively to generate sales and thereby more commission. It provides them with more options to bundle products together in the form of promotions. In summary, you will usually find Front-end (FE) functions wanting and promoting a lot of products, product variants and "*a SKU for everything*" approach to life.

The Back-End (BE) functions typically include all those functions that manage the product's fulfillment to the customer. Typical questions in the back of the mind of Back-end function manager are:

- *"How can I minimize the total cost of operations?"*
- *"How can I manage the lifecycle and after-sales support for so many products without hiring more resources?"*
- *"How can I get this order out the door to the customer on the date the customer needs it while minimizing my cost of getting that done?"*

While there are positives to having many products and product variants, there is an increased cost of product proliferation. Too many product variations can be unhealthy in two ways – they can have an adverse impact to top-line growth (the "Sales" number) and the "Total Cost" metric. One may wonder as to why would an excessive number of product offerings hurt top-line growth, because that seems counter-intuitive to the marketing mindset. One of the direct negatives of too many choices is the resulting customer confusion. If a new product is created for every small product differentiator (*even insignificant value differentiators*), then the company has created enough confusion in the minds of the end customer that can deflect the customer to a competitor's product. A walk down the aisle of the shampoo or toothpaste aisle at Wal-Mart is proof of this confusion and frustration that we face when it comes to "too many choices". Take the case of Procter & Gamble. When the company reduced the number of versions of Head & Shoulders shampoo from a staggering 26 to just 15, it experienced a 10% increase in sales. So, just more offerings in the form of products do not necessarily mean more sales. As a matter of fact, _the additional 11 SKUs of Head & Shoulders were essentially decreasing sales by 10%_!! This is a classic example of excessive SKUs creating excessive confusion thereby impacting top-line growth. The second reason why too many product variations are unhealthy goes with its negative impact to the "Total Cost" metric. Each product offering costs money to the company – from the sheer creation of the product to its maintenance by all the supporting functions in the organization. Engineering functions have to maintain the integrity of the product and its structure in engineering systems. Planning functions have to support the forecast and life-cycle management of the product in planning systems. The factories and other supporting functions like marketing and services have to also maintain the product in their respective systems. The net result is that a product costs a lot of money to sustain itself. Depending on the company size, culture & product attributes, the cost to maintain product can range anywhere from a few hundreds to many thousands of dollars. A good example of a company that suffered in its cost metric due to excessive SKUs is the Lego Group. The group lost money in four out of seven years from 1998 through 2004. The Lego Group was losing $337,000 in value every day. The primary reason was due to the complexity of its product line as manifested by a large number of SKUs. Just 30 products generated 80% of the sales. The company had 1500 SKUs, 11000 suppliers (*twice as many suppliers as Boeing*) and over 800 machines in its Danish factory!!! Capacity utilization was just 70% due to changing demands. The company then undertook a huge initiative to cut downs its Product/ SKU offering. Lego cut the colors in half and cut out many of the toys from its marketing offering. The cost of a SKU became a key factor in evaluating new products. The new culture and strategic moves resulted in increased profitability for the company.

As a young professional, it is important to understand the FE and BE functions and their inherent motivations that seem to operate in conflict. _Too many SKUs are costly & confusing to the customer and too few are offer less choices_. The sooner one can appreciate this delicate balance that an organization has to strive for and the underlying rationale behind the same, the more successful you will be in the long run. These are the kinds of strategic decisions that you as a professional need to be comfortable understanding and making in order to be successful. And the higher up you grow in an organization, the decisions are less "black and white" and more "grayish" in tones.

The "Process" advantage

Companies with good processes have a significant competitive advantage over those that do not. This should come as no surprise. We have seen many examples of companies becoming successful just by delivering the "same product" using a "different process". Amazon is a great example. The brick-and-mortar company, Barnes & Noble, pretty much ruled the industry of books. The company had mastered the supply chain of selling books through its huge chain of retail outlets. It had stopped worrying about any other competitor coming into this space until Amazon came on board. The end product is the same – books. The process was different – sell it online instead of a brick-and-mortar outlet. As I write this paragraph, Amazon has a market cap of $55 billion while Barnes and Noble is less than a billion dollars in market capitalization. Looking at it a bit differently, the "process differentiation" is worth $55 billion!.

Another great company that believes in the power of processes is Proctor & Gamble (P&G). The consumer goods giant is a strong believer in the philosophy that *"product innovation is a fragile advantage that can be easily copied through reverse engineering; while process innovation is much more robust and long-lasting"*. P&G, therefore, considers factory equipment design and development to be core strengths. Many more examples can be cited of companies that have become huge successes by playing the "process card". _You can become an instant success if you can re-engineer processes_. At the end of the day, the probability of a hugely successful product innovation is a lot lower than a process innovation. So, become a process expert. Read books on process re-engineering and how to use systems thinking effectively in redesigning value chains. You will soon discover that opportunities abound everywhere – from redesigning processes to save money to redesigning processes to develop a new competitive advantage that never existed before. The ability to quickly comprehend the dependencies between different activities and systems, flowchart the same and come up with a compellingly alternative way of achieving the organization's goals is a skill that is worth its weight in gold.

Tip 41: ***Read a good basic book on Management Accounting and understand the basic concepts***

Tip 42: ***Appreciate the fact that there is a lot of estimation in financial statements. The "Net Profit" reported in the Income Statement is also, in reality, just an estimate***

Tip 43: ***The creation of the EBITDA metric was driven primarily by an interest to truly understand how a company manages its operations by removing all "estimates" out of the puzzle***

<u>Tip 44</u>: Front-end functions like Marketing and Sales usually operate in "a SKU for everything" mentality. Back-end functions prefer fewer offerings to reduce the operational cost. Understanding the fine balance between "cost & confusion" vs. "choices" is key to a successful business strategy

<u>Tip 45</u>: Process is king, no matter what anyone says!! Product innovation is a fragile advantage that can be easily copied through reverse engineering; while process innovation is much more robust and long-lasting. You can become an instant success if you can re-engineer processes

Chapter 11

Brand "I" Management

"Distinct ... or Extinct" – Tom Peters

The power of branding

Branding is everything ... well, almost. Nothing captures the importance of branding than the quote *"Distinct ... Or Extinct"* by Tom Peters. If you are not distinct from your competition, you are just like a commodity and will become extinct with the passage of time. Branding is all about being distinct. It is about being different or being perceived differently by those who matter. This is precisely why two different persons doing the same job and almost the same quality can still be perceived differently because of how the minutest act was taken care of. In his best-selling book, *Purple Cow*, marketing guru Seth Godin writes:

"Remarkable people with remarkable careers seem

to switch jobs with far less effort. They don't even need a resume. Instead, they rely on sneezers who are quick to recommend them when openings come up". Remarkable people carry an excellent brand value because of the work they do, which is always distinct from the work the majority of people do. So, what exactly is your brand and how can make a fairly good self-assessment of the same? A simple way to think about your brand is to list the behaviors that you consistently do on a daily basis. Your brand is nothing but the list of your "consistent behaviors". If you are doing something consistently that is not in sync with the brand you wish to be, then you should seriously consider dropping that behavior.

When $1 is worth more than $25000

Take a look at a typical Fedex truck. Notice any difference as compared to any other truck on the road? The sharp eye will clearly notice that the Fedex trucks are relatively much cleaner, tidier and nicer looking. Why? Because Fedex took the words of Harvard marketing guru, Ted Levitt, pretty damn seriously. Levitt's theory was simple: *"If your product is tangible (plane, boat, car etc.), distinguish yourself from the herd by emphasizing intangibles (e.g. service). If your product is intangible (banking services, travel services), distinguish by emphasizing the tangible".* At the end of the day, Fedex is providing a service. It is an intangible service. So, while taking care of the intangibles is of paramount importance in order to survive, Fedex also realized that it has to distinguish itself also in the tangible space. The physical "truck" is part of the definition of tangibles. Therefore, it was clearly important that the truck stands out as unique and clean – all the time. This is also precisely why you as an entry-level professional should always stay one notch above the rest when it comes to dressing and style. Because, when there is a tie in service levels provided by entry-level professionals, the higher-ups start scratching the head for *"what else?"* type of differentiators. It is at these times that the $1 can of cotton starch that helped add the extra crease to your shirt is actually worth many thousands over. It can decide whether you get the promotion with the $25K raise or not!!

An emphasis on packaging

Being good or great from a talent perspective is one thing. However, success will rarely come to anyone who has not been packaged and presented well to showcase the talent. A lot about brand management is ultimately about "packaging management". I have never visited the showroom of a Mercedes-Benz but I can say with a lot of certainty that its showroom will be more impressive than that of a Kia for the simple reason that a Benz packaging has to reflect the Benz lifestyle. From a product perspective, both the cars will take you from point A to point B. The only exception is that one reflects a different "lifestyle" than the other.

A few years ago, the Washington Post conducted a social experiment to better understand the importance of perception, tastes and priorities. As part of the experiment, the famous violinist, Josh Bell, played incognito at the Washington DC Metro station on a cold January morning in the year 2007. He played a total of six Bach pieces for about 45 minutes with his violin that was worth $3.5 million dollars. In those forty five minutes, an estimated 2000 people went past him. His first dollar was earned after 4 minutes, thanks to a woman who threw it in the hat but did not stop to listen. A total of just 6 people stopped and listened for a short while and about 20 people gave money totaling about $32!!! Interestingly, the majority of the $32 came from one old lady who knew the genius behind the instrument. Contrast this to what happened just two days before when the famous violinist sold out a theater in Boston with seat prices averaging $100 in which Josh Bell makes close to $1000 a minute. The power of packaging is the difference between $60,000/hour and $32/hour. This, by no means, implies that every guy playing in the subway can earn $60,000/hour just by being packaged well. The talent is a pre-requisite. Nothing can steal the fact that Josh Bell is a genius and people are paying big money for his talent. However, what it does mean is that _excellent talent can become a total failure if it is not packaged and promoted correctly_. People associate your value based on the entire picture and not just one part of it. Moral of the story: _Focus on the presentation & packaging_!!

A lesson from Bollywood

Aamir Khan is one of the most successful stars from Indian cinema. As I write this chapter (early part of the year 2010), the last four films of the actor which were released over three consecutive years made a collective box office revenue of over Rs.590 crores in

Indian currency – roughly $120 million in US currency. In a recent interview, the actor quoted *"The two mistakes I made early on was signing nine films within six months of my debut and giving too much importance to scripts, not directors"*. The same applies to life in the corporate world. When translated to the life of a corporate professional, the director is the boss. _The importance of the role of your boss in influencing the progress of your career should never be underestimated_. While focusing on the script (the work itself) is important, it is of even more importance to understand who is in charge of your career – from giving you the sleek assignments and projects to showcasing you and your wins with the management layers above him. And, most importantly, working for a boss whom you admire and respect will also contribute to significant job satisfaction – a pre-requisite for performing at your peak.

Branding the Google way

When it comes to a brand success story, one of the finest ones is *Google*. A company and name that was relatively unknown about 15 years ago now finds itself as a proper transitive verb in the dictionary. If you could manage your brand image even a tenth as good as Google has, you could be a few rungs higher up the career ladder already. Why is Google so good? One of the many reasons is that Google takes criticisms and feedbacks from the end users very seriously. There is a story about an individual who kept emailing Google anonymously with a two-digit number. That's all his emails contained – a simple 2 digit number. If the number went up from his previous email, he would shoot an email again with a new number. After a lot of analysis, Google concluded that the number in the email reflected the number of words in their home page. If that number went up, it was a bad sign and enough to trigger an angry response from the user. The lesson for Google was simple: *Keep the number of words in the home page to a minimum. Keep the home page simple.* Google took the message seriously. Is it any surprise why you don't see too much crowding in the Google homepage? On the contrary, how much effort does the average individual put in the branding of his or her name? Not much. This is precisely why only a handful makes it to the top. It is the very few who take their brand images seriously. And, these select few watch out for constructive criticism and take the remedial measures sooner than later.

The state of emotional neutrality

One of the key attributes of successful people is that they rarely make decisions impulsively. The greater the impact of the decision, the more thought is put into the decision making process. No matter how pressing or urgent the matter at hand may be, it is important for you as a professional to allow a period of time to pass and compose yourself before pulling the trigger. In other words, _make decisions when you are in an emotionally neutral state_. Decisions made in a rash when your emotions are not in control will put you in a bad light as seen by others. You will be then be perceived as someone with a low tolerance level for stress. And, you will soon realize that perception is one of the biggest factors in corporate success.

Take the game of cricket. It can be one fast-paced game. A pace bowler can deliver balls at speeds averaging 90 mph. To be the on the receiving end of this and to be the best in the world is no easy feat. That's what Sachin Tendulkar is all about. The ace cricketer and great batsman stated the following in a recent interview: "_You have to allow your instincts to take over, trust me, your instincts are 99 per cent right but, you know, the older I get the more I realize how important your breathing is to good batting. By that I mean, if you focus on breathing and relaxing, you can force yourself into a_ *comfortable place to bat*". As you manage your career actively, you will come across many situations where you will be extremely frustrated with the events of the day. You will find employees reporting to you who are not pulling in their weight or you will find peers and even bosses who play dirty politics at times. This is all part of the overall package called "corporate world" – whether it be corporate America or corporate India or corporate Japan. The actual personalities may be different but the experiences are the same. Just as breathing is important to good batting, so is it important to good and successful corporate behavior. Before you react impulsively to a nasty email that points fingers at you or to some comment by a colleague in a meeting, it is best to take in a few deep breaths and calm down. Plan and implement the next action only after you have rationalized the step in a state of relaxation. There have been more screw-ups done in the corporate world due to a hasty action that could have been totally avoided if the person had taken the time to calm themselves down before deciding on the next logical step.

Perception – the silent killer

One of the biggest problems that you will face throughout your career is the inability to understand how others "perceive" of you as an individual. You're going to hear lots of feedback from peers and bosses in different forums – via performance evaluations or 360 degree feedbacks or even informal one-on-one conversations. If you are not that lucky to get feedback, it's even worse because you will never know what may potentially be the true cause of your career progression lag. No matter what, one point should be clear - *if you hear a certain piece of feedback consistently and you don't agree with it, it doesn't matter what you think*. Truth is, you're being perceived that way. And, if you are perceived the same way by the key decision makers who control your career progression, the chances are pretty low if the perception is not in sync with what you think of yourself. So, keep an open ear for any feedbacks and try to gauge how you are "truly" perceived. The less defensive you are, the more prepared you will be to such inputs and the greater the awareness you will have yourself. And, if the findings reveal one small annoying habit that can be easily dropped of your arsenal or one new easy habit that needs to be added to your arsenal for a quick move upwards, that by itself might be worth the effort. A simple example can help clarify this situation. A common tactic adopted by many is to remain silent when you truly agree with a speaker's viewpoint. The speaker may be your peer, boss or anyone for that matter. If you consistently speak up only when you disagree, then you set a perception that you are always being confrontational and oppositional to new viewpoints. This is because the various speakers have never seen you actively support or say "yes" to anything. The only images they have of you is when you said "no" and disagreed violently. A simple change of actively supporting a position that you like would neutralize that perception.

Jack Welch is a name known to everyone. He is considered to be one of the greatest CEOs that Corporate America has ever produced. In his book "Winning", Jack Welch writes *"Differentiation favors people who are energetic and extroverted and undervalues people who are shy and introverted, even if they are talented. I don't know if it is good or bad but the world generally favors people who are energetic and extroverted."* This highlights the importance of perception and branding. When people see you, do they see a shy, introverted and boring person? Or do they see you as someone who is full of energy, passion and drive? That's perception!!

Be assertive ... and aligned

One of Elizabeth Dole's quotes is also a personal favorite of mine ~ *"The President doesn't want yes-men and yes-women around him. When he says no, we all say no"*. In my opinion, the quote has some good relevance especially in the context of building a strong rapport with your boss. Like it or not, the universal rule to remember is that every boss (no matter what the position) has an ego that is a notch higher than those below him. If you have mastered the art of stroking his ego, you are pretty close to being the name on his succession plan. As part of this master plan, you need to know when to say "yes" and when to say "yes" and when to say "yes" to your boss. The simple answer is: *pretty much all the time.* Some people get confused with the quality of assertiveness and start to erroneously assume that saying "no" and "standing up on your feet against your boss" is a sign of being assertive. Bad move!! That position will be the quickest career checkmate. Your boss should get the feeling that you are assertive yet someone who will always stand by him and not go against him. If you have an opinion that is contrary to your boss, offer it in a way that is more like "feeding additional information for decision making"... but not actually making the decision on behalf of your boss or worse yet, against your boss's line of thinking.

<u>Moral of the story</u>: *The more you are aligned to your boss, the more the trust your boss has on you and the more you will get rewarded in time.*

From "scripts" to "opinion coalitions"

Organizations are complex hierarchies. No matter what jargon is used to describe the structures (flat, hybrid, matrix, horizontal, vertical, extremely flat etc.), the fact of the matter is that it is still a hierarchy at the end of the day. You have a boss, your boss has a boss until it reaches its natural end state being the CEO or President or Managing Director or whatever the title may be for the *numero uno* person. The most important lesson for a novice or mid-level professional to remember is that *<u>the decision making process at the higher levels of management is different than what happens at the lower levels</u>*. At the lower levels of an organization, the decisions and activities are "script driven". There are rules and procedures of how things get done. To a large extent, a lot of the decision making is automated or semi-automated so that the richness and fun of the job is lost. *"If X, then Y"* is the mode of operation at the lower levels. If you have mastered a lot more of these decision criteria than an average employee, then you have become a specialist. People will give you the importance – not for the leadership, but for the factual knowledge. The problem comes when after years of doing such a stellar job in *"If X, then Y"* type role, the employee begins to wonder why the career growth has come to a standstill. You are probably in a similar situation too. The solution for this dilemma is simple. *You need to get out of the roles where your factual knowledge is the sole reason for your paycheck*. Factual knowledge is cheap. Hence, it does not get you noticed and help you propel forward. If you wish to move ahead, you need to break away from this level and mode of decision making. *You need to get comfortable with* _decision-making under ambiguous conditions_. The biggest differentiator in the higher levels of management is that the decisions made at those levels are not "purely fact-based". Instead, decisions are weighted across multiple dimensions and frequently are _a result of opinion coalitions_. So, what may seem totally illogical to you at the current level of thinking may be perfectly logical at the higher levels of management because the process of arriving at decisions is completely different. The closer you get to that level of thinking and "opinion coalitions" mindset, the greater your chances of hitting a home run, or maybe many home runs.

Appreciating Sprezzatura

Sprezzatura is a beautiful Italian word. It sounds great for sure. But, more than that, it has a powerful meaning. It means "_a certain nonchalance, so as to conceal all art and make whatever one does or says appear to be without effort and almost without any_ *thought about it"*. It is _the ability to display an easy facility in accomplishing difficult actions which hides the conscious effort that went into them_. The very first image that came to me when I heard of the word was Roger Federer, whom I believe is the greatest tennis player of all time and one my personal favorites. Roger Federer displays Sprezzatura because every game he plays and wins is done with a grace and calmness that makes it seem like tennis is one simple and easy game. Roger can reach some of the almost impossible areas of the court and play some of the most amazing strokes that leave you in awe not because he did it but because he did it by hiding any conscious effort. That is what Sprezzatura is all about. The ability to display this quality is an important one as part of the Brand "I" initiatives because it is a key quality that many successful leaders constantly display. _Successful leaders are calm under stress_. The smartest managers and leaders achieve what they want by not putting a whole lot of "conscious" effort into it. Note the emphasis on the word "conscious". As a career conscious professional, try to embrace Sprezzatura. It has a key role in building the perception you need for corporate success.

Take a contrarian position

One of the key attributes of successful people in the corporate world is that they rarely repeat what other people have already stated. There is nothing original in repeating or just agreeing with someone. However, if you do not totally agree with the position of someone in the team, do not hold yourself back from taking on a contrarian position. The majority of good leaders like to see younger entry-level employees stand up on their feet and offer their opinion on something and argue against the conventional wisdom of the day. They like to see someone defend a position with passion and energy. Good leaders like to see you be "yourself". So, if you want to be seen positively by the top leaders of your organization, here are a few tips in random order:

- *Have a strong and original point of view.*
- *Do not focus on just imparting facts and figures. Information has no value.*
- *Do not just agree with someone ... take a contrarian position and defend it. Be yourself.*
- *Speak up!! And, speak a lot when a lot is at stake.*

Be unpredictable

Over the years, I have tried to observe many executives in meetings and note patterns in the way they think and act. One of the more interesting patterns that I see rather consistently among many of them is they are not predictable. *"Unpredictability" is the hallmark of successful leaders.* If you cannot keep others guessing to some extent as to what you will say or do, you are just "one of them" and you cannot afford to be "one of them" if you wish to be seen as someone "different". Being unpredictable does not mean you have to necessarily say something different for the sake of saying something different. It means that do not take positions too fast on any issue. Take your time. Use silence as a good weapon. Understand all the facts by active listening. And, finally, when the timing is just right and people least expect it .... Attack!! Ask the question that no one would have thought of. Say something that is profoundly insightful. Be different. Be unpredictable.

The "Speak Up-Shut Up" Flowchart

It is not surprising to see many professionals (even the so called experienced ones) lack the basic judgment around what is perhaps the most fundamental question around "Brand I" management – *"When should I speak up and when should I shut up?"*. This question becomes even more relevant when you are in meetings where decisions are being made and you do not have the luxury of time to come back later with your fresh perspective. You have to make the decision right then and there. Based on my experience, there is a very simplistic way to quickly arrive at the answer to this question. It is driven by the answer to the below two questions:

- *Is the topic at hand of importance to you?* In other words, do you really care about what is being debated? Does it personally affect you? Do you stand to lose something or gain something by speaking up and fighting for your position'? You have to be clear around "what personally affects" connotes in this reference and the degree to which it affects you.

2. Assuming that the answer to the first question is affirmative, *what are the odds of you winning it* if you spoke up and fought for it? Note that you do not even consider this question if the answer to the first question was not affirmative!!

A simple flowchart of this logic will help you decide at all times when to speak up and when to shut up.

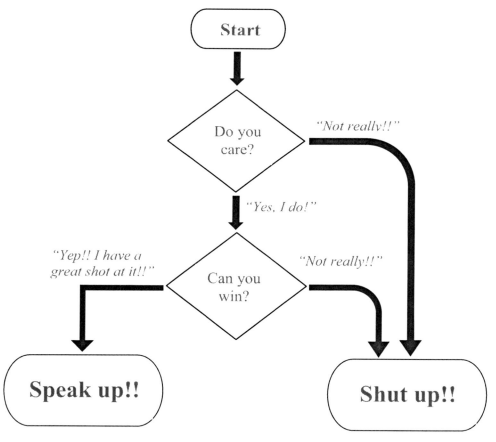

In summary, the logic is pretty simple. There are two scenarios that govern when to "Shut up!"

- You don't care!!
- You do care but the odds of winning are pretty low

No alibis please!!!

As you go through corporate life taking chances and risks, some failure is inevitable. What separates the star employees from the non-stars is how they react to failures. One of the most important rules that star employees operate by is the rule of *"No alibis"* – which means no failure justifications using a bunch of "If" statements. If you start justifying your failure using a statement like "If I had just one more month...." or "If I had just one more person in my team...." or "If that other team had delivered in time..." etc. etc...........Get the drift?

Be comfy looking dumb

One of the best books on leadership is *"Winning"* by Jack Welch. The book is a must-read book for every person who wishes to learn the trade secrets of leading from none other than the greatest leaders Corporate America has ever produced. One of my favorite parts in the book is how Mr. Welch distinguishes an individual contributor from that of a leader.

Quoting Jack Welch:

> "When you are an individual contributor, you try to have all the answers. That's your job – to be an expert. When you are a leader, your job is to have all the questions. _You have to be incredibly comfortable looking like the dumbest person in the room_. Leaders ask questions like "What if?", "Why not?" and "How come?". Questioning, however, is not enough. You have to make sure your questions unleash debate and raise issues that get action."

What an amazingly profound thought conveyed with such simplicity and clarity!! I wonder if the need to be "seen as an expert" is actually a product of our schooling system – a system that thrives on rewarding students with the right answers. Should schools change their methodology and start rewarding students with the right questions instead? Something to seriously ponder ....

Don't work for jerks

The management guru, Peter Drucker, once said "_I have yet to sit down with a manager, whatever his_ *level of job, who was not primarily concerned with his upward relations and upward communications"*. So, stop wondering why your boss spends so much time upwards and less time with you or downwards. <u>*The key to anyone's career progression lies with the higher-ups; not the people below*</u>. That is a fact. You cannot change that. In the book "It takes two", Author Gene Bocialetti states it beautifully: *"I'm not advising you to be holier-than-thou. Politics is normal. Compromise is eternal. But there are limits. For example: Don't work for people who are dishonest. Don't work with people who don't keep their word. Don't work with people who care only about themselves. Don't work with jerks. Life is too short."* You will be a lot more successful if you work for someone who also has your career goals as part of his agenda. If your current boss does not fit this requirement, it is a sign for you to hop. And, remember that *toxic bosses are not an endangered species!!*

Be Funny – The "haha" type

It goes without a doubt that employees like positive-spirited bosses. The bosses who carry a sense of humor around with them and showcase that there is more to life than just hitting the "revenues and margins" always have an edge over other bosses when it comes to "true followership". Research by Goleman and the Hay Group has found that within organizations, the most effective leaders were funny (*that is funny ha-ha, not funny strange*). These leaders had their employees laughing three times more often & being significantly more productive than their non-funny counterparts. That's a pretty significant difference by any measure. *"Humor, used skillfully, greases the management wheels"*, writes Fabio Sala in a research article published in the Harvard Business Review. The most effective executives deployed humor twice as often as the middle-of-the-pack managers.

Read a lot

I love to read – primarily non-fiction. I like to read books written by authors who offer a unique perspective. I have many favorites but a few definitely stand out. I still vividly remember the day in the early 90's when I was strolling in one of the aisles in a public library in the city of Dallas, Texas. My eyes fell on a book titled *"The Goal"* by Eliyahu Goldratt. The cover of the book isn't one of the most attractive ones and I do not think it has changed in the 25 years since it has been published. For some reason, I decided to check it out despite its not-so-attractive packaging. I finished reading the book the same day!! Not surprisingly, I have read every book of Dr. Goldratt. Another of my favorite authors has been marketing whiz, Seth Godin. Unlike Goldratt, Seth's books draw you to them like bees to a honeycomb starting from the cover of the book. Everything about Seth's works is magical. His style of writing is fabulous, his way of thinking is totally out-of-the-box and his way of getting the message across to the reader is simple and direct. I have been influenced a lot by Seth over the years. I encourage every reader who wishes to *"think differently"* and who wish to *"create a competitive differentiation"* read all of Seth's works. There are many others in my list of favorite authors including Ken Blanchard, Patrick Lencioni, Peter Senge and C.K.Prahalad to name a few. I encourage each of you as young professionals to read a lot of non-fiction books written by such fabulous writers. It helps you stay in the company of great minds. It can be the greatest source of inspiration and motivation in the midst of a corporate journey that is characterized by political peccadillos and more-than-occasional frustrations.

The management of your brand is not a trivial exercise. This is, perhaps, the most important chapter in this book. As part of your effort to renew and refine your brand image, please note below some of my tips:

Tip 46: **Be Distinct ... If not, you will be Extinct very soon**

Tip 47: **Put simply ... Your brand is what you do "consistently"**

Tip 48: **Excellent talent can become a total failure if it is not packaged and promoted correctly**

Tip 49: **The importance of the role of your boss in influencing the progress of your career should never be underestimated**

Tip 50: **If Google takes criticism seriously, shouldn't you and me?**

Tip 51: **Make big decisions in a state of emotional neutrality**

Tip 52: **The more you are aligned to your boss, the more the trust your boss has on you and the more you will get rewarded in time**

Tip 53: **Get comfortable with decision-making under ambiguous conditions**

Tip 54: **Make big decisions in a state of**

Tip 55: **Perception matters ... a lot!!**

Tip 56: **Appreciate the fact that the logic of decision making changes as you climb up the organization chart – from "pure objectivity" to "opinion coalitions"**

Tip 57: Embrace "Sprezzatura"

Tip 58: Take contrarian positions and defend them with passion

Tip 59: "Unpredictability" is the hallmark of many successful leaders

Tip 60: Remember when to "Speak Up" and when to just "Shut Up"

Tip 61: Do not use any alibis for your failures

Tip 62: Be extremely comfy looking dumb

Tip 63: Don't work for jerks or with jerks. Remember that toxic bosses are not an *endangered species!! Work for someone who also has <u>your</u> career goals as part of his or her agenda*

__Tip 64__: Remember that humor, when used skillfully, can grease the management wheels

Chapter 12

The back-pocket panacea

"There is some self-interest behind every friendship. There is no friendship without self-interests. This is a bitter truth" – Chanakya

I was debating whether to write this last chapter or not, but felt that it is important to bring closure to this book with a slightly more philosophical touch. As you know as much as I know, there are no guarantees to anything in life. Likewise, while I have tried to do justice in the first eleven chapters of this book by laying out a foundation for every new entrant to the corporate world, implementing the suggestions of these chapters by themselves <u>does not guarantee</u> anything. The tips outlined in the previous chapters can significantly increase you probability of career success; however they cannot offer you a 100% certainty of success. There will be many instances where you will find yourself in situations that are beyond your control. No matter how well you play your game, it is possible that your manager may still prefer your peer over you for the next promotion for reasons unknown that can never be logically explained. *The problem is not with having expectations or goals in life.* <u>*The bigger problem is how we react when our goals are not achieved in life*</u>. We can never control the real outcome but we sure can control how we react to those outcomes, whether they are favorable or unfavorable from our perspective. In the book "Are you ready to succeed?", author Srikumar S. Rao writes a beautiful statement and I quote ~ *"Recognize that if ego gratification is the major component of your motivation, the Universe is unlikely to play ball with you"*. So, while you go through the motions of your career journey, always remember that the world is not revolving around your goals. The entire subject of Economics revolves primarily around one premise that people will always act and take positions that are aligned to their self-interests. If you do not accept this premise, you will be doomed for failure and regrets. So, the last takeaway of this book, which I also term as the "back-pocket panacea", is as below:

My back-pocket panacea

- *I realize that every action by every person has a self-directed motive. That is a universal fact of life.*

- *I will not sweat over outcomes that I have no control or influence over.*

- *The only thing that I truly have total power and control over is "my reactions to life's outcomes".*
  No one can take away that power from me.

References

Listed below are the books and articles that have been an integral part of making my book a reality. I want to convey my sincere thanks and gratitude to all the below authors, who's works have been borrowed in small amounts to emphasize a key point without stealing the thunder of what their books have to offer in totality. I encourage every reader to read the below works to improve your perspective and knowledge because each one is a gem in its own right. If anyone has been left out inadvertently, it is an honest mistake on my part that will be rectified in my next edition.

- Bob Brier & Jean-Pierre Houdin: "The Secret of the Great Pyramid", 1st edition, 2009

- Joe Kita. "Bounce Back from Anything". Reader's Digest, May 2009 edition

- Howard Gardner. "Multiple Intelligences: New Horizons in Theory and Practice". Basic Books, July 2006 edition

- "SONY Lost in Transformation" by Richard Siklos in Fortune Magazine, July 6, 2009

- "Strengths based leadership" by Tom Rath & Barry Conche

- "Yes!: 50 scientifically proven ways to be persuasive" by Robert Cialdini et al

- "Children of Heaven", Foreign Film

- Gene Boccialetti. "It takes two – Managing yourself when working with bosses and other authority figures"

- Kaj Grichnik et al: "MAKE or BREAK – How Manufacturers can leap from Decline to Revitalization"

- Peter Senge. "The Fifth Discipline"

- Peggy Klaus. "The Hard Truth about Soft Skills", Harper Collins

- Seth Godin. "Purple Cow"

- Christopher Witt. "Real Leaders don't do PowerPoint"

- Srikumar S. Rao "Are you ready to succeed?"

- Daniel H. Pink - "A Whole New Mind"

- Jim Hauden - "The Art of Engagement"

- Jeremy Gutsche – "Exploiting Chaos"

- Ori Brafman & Rod A. Beckstrom – "The Starfish and the Spider", Penguin Books, 2006

Appendix

"Otaku" Discovery Sheet

My name:
Today's date :

Things I am good at and I like	Things I am good at but I don't like	Things that I am not good at and I don't like

"Companies I love or admire"

My name:
Today's date :

My Rank for the company	Company Name	Why I love this company?

"*Otaku*" Discovery Sheet

My name: Ram
Today's date : August 22, 2010

Things I am good at and I like	Things I am good at but I don't like	Things that I am not good at and I don't like
Strategic Thinking	Tactical execution	Routine type work with no creativity
Writing skills	Too much detail	Non-intellectual assignments
Marketing a concept		Working without a mission or end-goal
Communicating to teams		
Building effective relationships		
Delegating		
Driving people to execute successfully		

"Companies I love or admire"

My name: Ram
Today's date : August 22, 2010

My Rank for the company	Company Name	Why I love this company?
1	Coca-Cola	Superb taste, Global brand name & I just love Coke!!!
2	Toyota	Fantastic cars, Reliable quality & I have never had any major problems
3	Apple	Really "cool" innovation
4	Wal-Mart	Value shopping experience. I just feel that the company takes care of negotiating the right price on my behalf with the suppliers.
5	Home Depot	I can't think of any other shop that can solve all my home related problems under one roof. Plus, I just love walking through the aisles.

About the Author

Ram Iyer is a management professional with a Fortune 100 company in the United States of America. He has a diverse experience in the automotive, consumer electronics and technology sectors. Over a career span of roughly two decades, Ram has held positions in engineering, operations management, project management, strategic advisory roles, process re-engineering and people management.

Ram was born and raised in the city of Mumbai where he earned his Bachelors in Engineering from the University of Mumbai passing with Distinction and a University rank holder. After a short stint in corporate India, he moved to the United States to pursue a Master of Science in Industrial Engineering. After a 6 year stint in corporate America, he went to school again to pursue a Master's in Business Administration.

For any comments or feedback, please contact the author directly at *thecareerjourney@gmail.com*

CPSIA information can be obtained at www.ICGtesting.com
226272LV00014B/11/P

9 781449 918392